# The "Babel" that was Enron
## Allen Schery

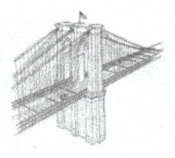

Brooklyn Bridge Books

Copyright 2025 by Allen Schery

All rights reserved.

No portion of this book may be reproduced in any form without written permission from the publisher or author, except as permitted by U.S. copyright law.

# Contents

| | |
|---|---|
| Preface | V |
| 1. The Corporate and Cultural Context of Enron | 1 |
| 2. Origins and Growth of Enron | 16 |
| 3. Key Players and Their Roles | 28 |
| 4. The Mechanics of Fraud and Deception | 34 |
| 5. Agency Behavior and Corporate Corruption | 48 |
| 6. The Systemic Roots of Enron's Collapse | 61 |
| 7. Internal Corporate Culture and Leadership Failures | 75 |
| 8. Regulatory and Oversight Results for Enron | 88 |
| 9. The Collapse of Enron | 97 |
| 10. Sarbanes Oxley Act and Regulatory Reform | 120 |
| 11. The Anthropological and Psychological Dimensions of Corporate Failure | 145 |
| 12. Lessons Learned and Forward Outlook | 180 |
| About the Author | 195 |

Bibliography 198
Index 228
Endnotes 238

# Preface

The Enron scandal remains etched as a profound cautionary tale in corporate history, its reverberations reshaping financial markets, regulatory frameworks, and corporate governance worldwide. Yet this book aims to transcend the familiar chronicle of collapse, inviting readers into a complex interdisciplinary exploration of the human, cognitive, cultural, and systemic forces that underpinned Enron's rise and catastrophic fall.

At the heart of this journey lies philosophical anthropology—an inquiry into human nature, cognition, and morality as products of deep evolutionary and cultural processes. Human ethics can be envisioned as intricate "mind paintings," layered compositions shaped over hundreds of thousands of years, born from the interplay of biology, cognition, social organization, culture, and history. The moral canvas began roughly 250,000 years ago in the African savannas, where survival depended on vigilance, cooperation, and social cohesion—the first brushstrokes of fairness, generosity, and mutual protection.

This evolutionary backdrop provides the foundation for understanding how human cognition and morality are wired to create and sustain ethical life. Practices like sentinel awareness—rotations of vigilant care among group members—and social leveling mechanisms to temper power demonstrate that ethics is neither fixed nor abstract but rooted deeply in our biological architecture and social environments. Comparative primatology reveals continuity with chimpanzees and bonobos, whose political alliances and empathy provide wild galleries of shared human pigments.

Building upon this foundation, cognitive science and neuroscience illuminate mechanisms through which morals are fixed and persist. The illusory truth effect, emotional arousal from ritual, and motivation for cognitive harmony all function as varnishes on this moral painting, embedding ethical conduct in brain tissue and social practice. Meanwhile, tribalism delineates borders that both protect and divide, framing moral murals in distinctive colors of language, rites, and culture.

The pluralistic nature of ethics—the layering of universal "base pigments" like fairness and empathy beneath diverse, context-rooted cultural "brushstrokes"—frames our perspective on morality and corporate ethics alike. While moral relativism suggests all codes are equally valid, philosophical pluralism acknowledges diversity yet insists on a shared floor permitting cross-cultural critique, dialogue, and aspiration toward justice. This synthesis draws from the works of Rawls, Haidt, Appiah, and others, bridging constructs of universal moral capacities with culturally specific expressions.

Epistemologically, this book integrates multiple fields to decode Enron's story and its lessons for the future:

Philosophical Anthropology offers insight into the complex weave of human nature, cognition, culture, and morality informing corporate behavior.

Cognitive Science and Neuroscience reveal the biological substrates of cognition, group conformity, moral emotion, and rationalization explaining how individuals and groups may enable deception.

Systems Theory uncovers the feedback loops and interdependencies within corporate and regulatory networks where small failures amplify catastrophically. Legal and Economic Epistemologies dissect frameworks of knowledge, incentives, and governance that structured opportunities and blind spots for fraud.

This multidisciplinary epistemic toolkit enables us to move beyond simplistic blame or legalistic recitations to understand how Enron's tragic story was authored by factors both human and systemic, proximate and ultimate.

As the book unfolds, it traces the historical and cultural contexts, scrutinizes fraud mechanisms and key actors, deciphers regulatory breakdowns, and ventures philosophical reflections on cognition, ethics, and human nature. Finally, it looks forward to systemic and technological innovations promising more transparent, ethical futures in corporate governance.

Through this text, readers are invited to not only learn what happened at Enron but to grapple with why it happened—how cognitive biases intertwine with cultural narratives, how moral defaults can be subverted in competitive societies, and how interdisciplinary insight might help erect more resilient structures of trust and accountability.

Welcome to this meticulous and multidisciplinary journey into one of the most consequential corporate sagas of our age.

# Chapter One
## The Corporate and Cultural Context of Enron

The Enron scandal, a watershed moment in American corporate history, unfolded against a backdrop of profound transformation within the U.S. economic and regulatory landscape of the 1990s. To comprehend the magnitude and underlying causes of Enron's dramatic rise and catastrophic fall, it is essential to examine the broader corporate and cultural context that shaped not only the company's trajectory but also the mindset of its leadership, employees, shareholders, and regulators. The 1990s were a decade characterized by soaring economic optimism, fierce competition, and an increasingly deregulated marketplace where free-market ideology reigned supreme. This vibrant yet volatile environment set the stage for both innovation and ethical lapses, casting a long shadow over corporate governance and business ethics that would culminate in one of the most infamous scandals in financial history.

Throughout the 1990s, the United States enjoyed robust economic growth, powered by technological advances, globalization, and buoyant financial markets. The stock market reached unprecedented heights, with the Dow Jones climbing from 2,633 in 1990 to over 11,000 by 2000, while venture capital investment proliferated, fueling the expansion of startups and established firms alike. Deregulation became a guiding principle for policymakers aspiring to unleash entrepreneurial energy and market efficiency, reflecting what economists call the "efficient market hypothesis"—the belief that markets naturally self-correct and allocate resources optimally when left unimpeded by government interference. A central tenet of this philosophy was the belief that less government interference would allow businesses to operate more dynamically, fostering innovation and profitability. This approach was embodied in landmark legislative changes such as the passage of the Energy Policy Act of 1992, which deregulated portions of the energy market, and the Telecommunications Act of 1996, which opened telecommunications markets to competition. While these reforms aimed to encourage competition and consumer benefits, they also weakened the safeguards traditionally imposed on corporate conduct and financial reporting, creating loopholes that would later be exploited with devastating consequences.

Critics might argue that deregulation was a necessary response to inefficient government-controlled markets, and they would be partially correct—deregulation did spur innovation and competition in many sectors. However, the philosophical anthropological perspective reveals a deeper issue: human cognitive architecture, evolved for small-group cooperation and immediate survival challenges, proved inadequate for managing the complex, abstract financial systems that deregulation unleashed. The sentinel awareness that served early humans well in scanning savannas for predators was ill-suited for detecting sophisticated financial engineering and multi-layered corporate structures. This cognitive mismatch between evolved psychology and modern market complexity created vulnerabilities that opportunistic actors could exploit.

Enron was a quintessential product of this deregulated era. Originally founded in 1985 through the merger of Houston Natural Gas and InterNorth, it ingeniously transformed itself from a regional natural gas pipeline company into a global energy trading behemoth, leveraging deregulated markets to expand into commodities trading, broadband, water services, and other ventures. The company's revenue growth was staggering—from $9.2 billion in 1995 to $100.8 billion in 2000, a more than tenfold increase that made it the seventh-largest company in the United States by revenue. The business environment fostered by deregulation encouraged companies to explore creative financial strategies and complex instruments for risk management and profit maximization. However, these innovations also introduced opacity and complexity, making it increasingly difficult for investors, regulators, and even internal stakeholders to scrutinize the true financial health of firms like Enron. The company's rapid growth was fueled by aggressive risk-taking and a relentless drive for market dominance, hallmarks of the broader ethos permeating corporate America at the time.

From a systems theory perspective, Enron's structure exemplified what complexity scientists call "emergent complexity"—simple deregulatory rules produced unpredictably complex corporate behaviors that no single regulator or oversight mechanism could effectively monitor. The company created over 2,800 subsidiaries, with more than 30 percent located in offshore tax havens, creating a labyrinthine structure that defied traditional regulatory oversight. This structural complexity was not accidental but strategic, designed to exploit regulatory gaps and create information asymmetries that benefited insiders at the expense of external stakeholders.

The cultural ethos dominating the corporate landscape during the 1990s valorized aggressive competition and the relentless pursuit of financial success—a "win at all costs" mentality that reflected deeper evolutionary and psychological patterns. Success was not merely measured in profits but was often conflated with moral virtue and social worth, echoing what anthropologists recognize as "prestige competition"—the drive for status and recognition that has characterized human societies for millennia. This competitive spirit transcended the boardroom, reflecting broader societal values that celebrated individual achievement, entrepreneurial audacity, and the acquisition of wealth as markers of success and personal merit. The "American Dream" ideology, with its emphasis on individual success through merit and effort, provided cultural legitimacy for increasingly aggressive business practices.

Within Enron, this ethos manifested through a high-pressure performance culture that cognitive scientists would recognize as a breeding ground for moral disengagement and cognitive dissonance. Executives and employees alike were incentivized through stock options and bonuses tied directly to short-term financial results, creating what economists call "moral hazard"—situations where individuals have incentives to take risks because they don't bear the full consequences of failure. The company adopted ruthless performance metrics, such as the "rank and yank" system pioneered by General Electric's Jack Welch, where the lowest-performing 10 percent of employees were routinely terminated. This system cultivated an environment of zero tolerance for underperformance and dissent, effectively eliminating internal checks on risky or unethical behavior.

Under the leadership of figures like Jeffrey Skilling, who championed a market-driven business model rooted in neoclassical economic theory, Enron's corporate culture grew increasingly cutthroat. Skilling, who held an MBA from Harvard Business School and had worked as a McKinsey consultant, brought a data-driven, analytical approach that viewed business as a series of mathematical optimizations rather than a social enterprise with ethical obligations. His vision embraced risk-taking and innovation but often at the expense of ethical considerations, reflecting what philosophers call "instrumental rationality"—the pursuit of efficiency in achieving goals without questioning the goals themselves. The corporate atmosphere was charged with a sense of invincibility, driven by the belief that skillful market manipulation and financial engineering could yield unbounded returns. This mindset, however, subordinated traditional business ethics and transparent governance to a relentless chase for profit and stock price appreciation. The energy within the company was electric yet perilous, with loyalty to corporate goals often overriding loyalty to truth or legal compliance.

Neuroscientific research on decision-making under pressure helps explain how this environment influenced behavior. High-stakes, competitive environments trigger the release of stress hormones like cortisol and adrenaline, which can impair the prefrontal cortex's ability to engage in careful ethical reasoning while enhancing the limbic system's focus on immediate rewards. This neurological response, adaptive for short-term survival challenges, becomes maladaptive in complex business environments where long-term consequences and ethical considerations should guide decision-making.

Embedded within this cultural milieu was a pervasive moral relativism, a climate where bending or outright breaking ethical rules became rationalized as necessary for competitive advantage. Ethical principles were not absent but were fluid and adaptable, subordinated to the overarching goal of business success—what anthropologists recognize as "situational ethics" common in competitive environments. This relativism was reinforced by the belief that the marketplace rewarded ingenuity and entrepreneurial spirit, and that conventional moral frameworks could be adjusted or sidelined in pursuit of innovation and growth. This worldview gave rise to a culture where accounting tricks, off-balance-sheet entities, and complex financial instruments were not only accepted but celebrated as cutting-edge methods. The pervasive rationalization encapsulated in the mentality "the end justifies the means" permeated the company's leadership mindset, obscuring the lines between legal compliance and deceit, between innovation and manipulation.

The psychological mechanisms underlying this moral flexibility can be understood through Leon Festinger's theory of cognitive dissonance and Albert Bandura's concept of moral disengagement.

Cognitive dissonance occurs when individuals hold conflicting beliefs or when their actions contradict their stated values, creating psychological tension that they seek to resolve. At Enron, employees and executives experienced dissonance between their personal ethical beliefs and the pressure to achieve financial targets through questionable means. To reduce this discomfort, they engaged in moral disengagement—psychological processes that allow individuals to behave unethically while maintaining their sense of moral identity. These processes include euphemistic labeling (calling fraud "aggressive accounting"), advantageous comparison ("everyone in the industry does it"), and diffusion of responsibility ("I was just following orders").

The consequences of deregulation and moral relativism were compounded by systemic weaknesses in regulatory oversight and institutional governance that reflected broader changes in American political economy. The reforms of the 1980s and 1990s, while designed to facilitate market freedom, also dismantled many traditional protections that had guarded against corporate excess and fraud since the New Deal era. The Private Securities Litigation Reform Act of 1995 imposed stricter requirements for shareholder litigation, unintentionally making it more difficult to challenge corporate misconduct by raising the bar for proving securities fraud. This legislation, passed with bipartisan support during the Clinton administration, reflected the era's faith in market self-regulation and suspicion of litigation as a regulatory mechanism.

At the same time, the Securities and Exchange Commission (SEC) struggled with limited resources and expertise, receiving only modest budget increases even as the markets they were supposed to regulate grew exponentially in size and complexity. The SEC's staff of approximately 3,000 was responsible for overseeing markets worth trillions of dollars and thousands of public companies, creating what regulatory scholars call "enforcement gaps"—areas where illegal behavior is unlikely to be detected or prosecuted. Compounding this regulatory vulnerability was the compromised position of auditing firms, particularly Arthur Andersen, which provided both auditing and consulting services to Enron in clear violation of the independence principles that should govern external auditing. Andersen earned $52 million from Enron in 2000—$25 million for auditing services and $27 million for consulting—creating obvious conflicts of interest that undermined their effectiveness as financial watchdogs.

From a network theory perspective, these regulatory failures created what complexity scientists call "systemic risk"—risks that emerge from the interconnections and feedback loops within the financial system rather than from any single institution. Enron's web of relationships with auditors, analysts, rating agencies, banks, and regulators created a system where failure in one node (audit independence) could cascade through the entire network, ultimately threatening the stability of energy markets and investor confidence more broadly.

At a psychological and cultural level, the corporate environment fostered mechanisms such as groupthink, conformity pressures, and cognitive dissonance that inhibited critical scrutiny and encouraged collective denial of uncomfortable truths. Social psychologist Irving Janis's concept of "groupthink" describes how cohesive groups, especially those under pressure and led by directive leaders, can make irrational decisions by suppressing dissent and failing to critically evaluate alternatives. At Enron, the combination of high-pressure performance metrics, charismatic leadership, and a culture of secrecy created textbook conditions for groupthink. Employees and executives absorbed the dominant narratives of success and invulnerability, often rationalizing unethical conduct to preserve group cohesion and personal cognitive harmony. This rationalization was reinforced by a culture that valued loyalty to corporate objectives and punished whistleblowing and dissent through mechanisms ranging from social ostracism to termination and legal intimidation.

The collective illusion of infallibility, bolstered by charismatic leaders like Kenneth Lay and Jeffrey Skilling and rising stock prices that seemed to validate all decisions, created a self-reinforcing shield against external criticism and internal ethical reflection. Anthropological research on leadership cults helps explain this dynamic—charismatic leaders who promise extraordinary rewards can induce followers to suspend normal ethical judgment and rational evaluation, particularly when the promised rewards seem to be materializing. Enron's stock price rose from $10 per share in 1990 to over $90 per share in 2000, providing powerful validation for leadership decisions and creating what psychologists call "confirmation bias"—the tendency to seek information that confirms existing beliefs while ignoring contradictory evidence.

The entrepreneurial risk-taking that fueled Enron's spectacular rise also assumed a reckless dimension that reflected deeper cognitive biases and structural incentive problems. The company's embrace of derivatives, special purpose entities (SPEs), and mark-to-market accounting represented innovations that provided short-term competitive advantages but also introduced significant moral hazard and financial opacity. Derivatives, which Warren Buffett famously called "financial weapons of mass destruction," allowed Enron to take massive speculative positions while keeping the associated risks off its balance sheet. SPEs, ostensibly independent entities that could purchase assets from Enron and assume associated debts, were actually controlled by Enron executives like Andrew Fastow, creating undisclosed conflicts of interest and hidden liabilities.

Mark-to-market accounting, in particular, allowed Enron to record projected profits immediately upon contract signing, irrespective of actual cash flows, contributing to a distorted picture of corporate health. This accounting method, while legal and appropriate for some trading operations, was extended by Enron to long-term contracts where future performance was highly uncertain. The result was that Enron could book decades of projected profits immediately, creating the illusion of consistent growth even when actual business performance was declining. This encouraged speculative ventures and risk-taking that disconnected the company's financial reporting from its economic realities, creating what economists call "earnings management"—the practice of using accounting flexibility to create the appearance of smooth, predictable earnings growth.

These risky behaviors aligned closely with the compensation structures within Enron, where executives and employees were rewarded based on stock performance and short-term results, creating profound incentives to prioritize financial engineering over sustainable business practices. CEO Jeffrey Skilling received total compensation of $132 million in 2000, most of it in stock options that would only have value if the stock price continued to rise. This created powerful incentives to maintain the appearance of growth and profitability regardless of underlying business fundamentals—a classic example of what agency theorists call "moral hazard."

Additionally, the broader societal values of the 1990s further shaped the corporate narrative in ways that made Enron's eventual collapse both more likely and more damaging. The "American Dream," emphasizing individualism, achievement, and economic mobility, reinforced the cultural license for aggressive capitalist pursuits. The socio-political context, marked by rapid globalization and technological innovation, raised the stakes for companies competing on an increasingly complex international stage while simultaneously creating new opportunities for regulatory arbitrage and tax avoidance through offshore subsidiaries. The end of the Cold War had seemingly validated free-market capitalism over state-directed alternatives, creating what political scientist Francis Fukuyama called "the end of history"—a sense that market-based democracy represented the final form of human social organization.

Enron's story, for a time, exemplified the promise of this new economic era, embodying the ideals of innovation, competitiveness, and wealth creation that captivated public imagination. The company was regularly featured on the covers of business magazines, won numerous awards for corporate innovation, and was consistently ranked among the most admired companies in America by Fortune magazine. Kenneth Lay became a prominent figure in Republican politics, while Jeffrey Skilling was celebrated as a visionary business leader who had created new markets and business models. When the façade of success crumbled, however, it exposed the moral and systemic frailties underpinning this brave new corporate world.

The speed and magnitude of Enron's collapse—from a market capitalization of $74 billion to bankruptcy in a matter of months—revealed the fragility of confidence-based business models and the dangers of excessive financial leverage. The company's bankruptcy filing in December 2001 was then the largest in U.S. history, wiping out $74 billion in shareholder value and eliminating 20,000 jobs while calling into question the entire system of corporate governance, financial reporting, and regulatory oversight that had allowed such a massive fraud to develop undetected.

From an interdisciplinary perspective, Enron's collapse can be understood as a convergence of evolutionary psychology, cognitive science, systems theory, economics, and sociology. Human beings, evolved for small-group cooperation and immediate survival challenges, proved vulnerable to the complex, abstract incentive structures of modern corporations. Cognitive biases that served our ancestors well—such as overconfidence, in-group loyalty, and the tendency to discount distant future consequences—became liabilities in corporate environments where success required careful risk assessment, independent judgment, and long-term thinking. The deregulated economic environment of the 1990s amplified these vulnerabilities by removing traditional constraints on risk-taking while creating powerful incentives for short-term performance.

In sum, the corporate and cultural context of Enron was a nexus of deregulation, aggressive capitalism, moral relativism, and psychological mechanisms that combined to foster an environment ripe for ethical breakdown. To understand Enron's collapse as a mere consequence of a few rogue executives is to overlook the systemic and cultural pathologies deeply embedded in the era's business landscape. The scandal emerged from the intersection of human cognitive limitations, misaligned incentive structures, regulatory capture, and cultural values that prioritized individual success over collective welfare. The following chapters will delve into these dimensions in greater detail, offering a multilayered analysis of how corporate culture, cognitive biases, regulatory failures, and evolving moral frameworks intersected to produce one of the most notorious corporate scandals in history, while also examining how these same dynamics continue to shape corporate behavior and regulatory challenges in the contemporary business environment.

# Chapter Two
## Origins and Growth of Enron

The genesis of Enron Corporation represents one of the most compelling examples of how visionary leadership, market deregulation, and corporate ambition can converge to create both spectacular success and catastrophic failure. To understand Enron's eventual collapse, it is essential to examine the company's origins and early growth trajectory, which established the cultural, organizational, and strategic foundations that would later enable its fraudulent practices. The story begins with Kenneth Lay, a charismatic economist and energy executive whose vision of transforming the energy industry through financial innovation would reshape an entire sector. Lay's early leadership established a corporate culture that prized aggressive risk-taking, financial engineering, and rapid growth—characteristics that would later be weaponized by Jeffrey Skilling and others to construct an elaborate facade of prosperity built on deception.

Kenneth Lee Lay, born in 1942 in rural Missouri to a Baptist minister father, embodied many quintessential American values: hard work, entrepreneurial ambition, and an unwavering belief in the power of free markets. His early life, marked by modest circumstances and strong moral foundations, would later create a profound irony given his role in one of America's greatest corporate scandals. After earning a bachelor's degree in economics from the University of Missouri and later a Ph.D. in economics from the University of Houston, Lay embarked on a career that would take him through various roles in the energy sector, including significant positions in both government and private companies. His academic background in economics, combined with his deep understanding of energy markets, positioned him perfectly to capitalize on the deregulatory trends that would transform the industry in the 1980s and 1990s.

Lay's journey to founding Enron began in earnest when he became CEO of Houston Natural Gas (HNG) in 1984, just as the natural gas industry was beginning to experience the early stages of deregulation. The 1970s energy crises had exposed the vulnerabilities of America's regulated energy system, creating political momentum for market-based solutions that would theoretically provide more efficient resource allocation and consumer benefits. Lay recognized that deregulation would fundamentally alter the competitive landscape of the energy industry, creating opportunities for companies that could adapt quickly to new market realities. His vision extended beyond traditional pipeline operations to encompass a more dynamic, trading-oriented business model that would treat energy as a financial commodity rather than merely a physical resource.

The actual founding of Enron occurred through a complex merger in 1985 between Houston Natural Gas and the much larger Omaha-based InterNorth, a transaction that exemplifies the opportunistic and sometimes predatory nature of corporate dealmaking during the 1980s. InterNorth, facing the threat of hostile takeover by corporate raiders, sought to defensively increase its size and debt load through strategic acquisitions. The merger terms were surprisingly favorable to the smaller HNG, partly due to Lay's negotiating skills and partly due to InterNorth's desperate circumstances. Despite being the acquired company, Lay managed to gain control of the combined entity's board of directors and ultimately became CEO, demonstrating the political acumen and strategic thinking that would characterize his leadership style.

The newly formed company, initially called HNG InterNorth before being renamed Enron in 1986, faced immediate challenges that would test Lay's vision and management capabilities. The natural gas market was experiencing a supply glut that depressed prices and put many of Enron's long-term gas contracts underwater, creating significant financial pressures. Management of the combined entity proved difficult, riddled with internal politics and cultural clashes between the two merged organizations. As a public company, Enron faced intense pressure from Wall Street to demonstrate consistent earnings growth, a pressure that would later contribute to the aggressive accounting practices that became central to its scandal.

From a philosophical anthropological perspective, Lay's early leadership reflected deeply embedded human tendencies toward optimism bias and overconfidence—cognitive patterns that served early humans well in small-group environments but can become liabilities in complex modern organizations. Lay's unwavering belief in deregulation and market efficiency reflected what behavioral economists call "motivated reasoning," where individuals seek information that confirms their existing beliefs while discounting contradictory evidence. His charismatic personality and ability to inspire followers also demonstrated classic patterns of alpha-male leadership that anthropologists observe across cultures, but which can become problematic when combined with modern corporate structures that concentrate enormous power in individual leaders.

The transformation of Enron from a traditional pipeline company into an energy trading powerhouse began in earnest with the arrival of Jeffrey Keith Skilling in 1990. Skilling, a Harvard MBA and former McKinsey & Company consultant, brought a fundamentally different perspective to the energy business that would revolutionize both Enron and the broader industry. Unlike the engineers and pipeline operators who had traditionally dominated energy companies, Skilling approached the business through the lens of financial theory and market analytics. His breakthrough insight was elegantly simple yet profound: transform Enron from a company that owned and operated physical assets into one that traded energy contracts and managed financial risk.

Skilling's background at McKinsey had exposed him to cutting-edge theories about market efficiency, risk management, and organizational design that were beginning to transform corporate America during the 1980s and 1990s. His consulting experience had also given him a particular worldview that valued intellectual analysis over operational expertise, complex financial engineering over straightforward business models, and rapid transformation over gradual evolution. This perspective, while innovative and potentially valuable, also contained the seeds of Enron's eventual destruction, as it prioritized abstract financial metrics over underlying business fundamentals and created a culture that celebrated complexity for its own sake.

The "Gas Bank" concept that Skilling developed in the early 1990s represented a genuine innovation in energy markets that demonstrated both his intellectual capabilities and the potential benefits of applying financial theory to commodity businesses. By buying gas supply contracts from producers and selling them to consumers while managing the associated price and delivery risks, Enron could generate profits from the spread between buying and selling prices while providing valuable services to both sides of the market. This business model required sophisticated risk management capabilities and deep understanding of both physical energy markets and financial derivatives, skills that Enron would develop over the following decade.

Skilling's transformation of Enron's corporate culture proved even more significant than his business model innovations. He systematically recruited top graduates from elite MBA programs, creating what he called an "intellectual meritocracy" that valued analytical prowess, competitive intensity, and financial performance above traditional business virtues like operational excellence, customer service, or ethical conduct. The "rank and yank" performance management system that he implemented, borrowed from General Electric's Jack Welch, created an intensely Darwinian environment where employees were rated against each other every six months, with the bottom 15-20 percent facing termination.

From a cognitive science perspective, Skilling's management approach created conditions ripe for the psychological phenomena that would later enable Enron's fraudulent practices. High-pressure competitive environments trigger stress responses that impair the prefrontal cortex's ability to engage in careful ethical reasoning while enhancing the limbic system's focus on immediate rewards and threat avoidance. The rank-and-yank system also fostered in-group/out-group dynamics that anthropologists recognize as fundamental to human social organization but which can become toxic in corporate environments. Employees learned to prioritize loyalty to their immediate team and supervisor over broader organizational or societal values, creating the conditions for collective rationalization of unethical behavior.

Skilling's hiring of Andrew Fastow in 1990 represents one of the most fateful personnel decisions in corporate history, as Fastow would later become the architect of the special purpose entities (SPEs) that enabled Enron's massive accounting fraud. Fastow, a Northwestern University MBA with a background in finance, quickly distinguished himself through his ability to create complex financial structures that appeared to reduce risk while actually concentrating it in hidden and dangerous ways. His rise through Enron's ranks demonstrated both the company's meritocratic culture and its growing emphasis on financial engineering over fundamental business operations.

The organizational culture that emerged under Skilling's leadership fostered both innovation and opacity in ways that would prove critical to understanding Enron's later scandals. The company's emphasis on intellectual capital over physical assets led to increasingly abstract business models that were difficult for outsiders—and even many insiders—to understand or evaluate. This opacity was initially seen as a competitive advantage, as it made it difficult for competitors to replicate Enron's strategies, but it later became a tool for concealing fraudulent practices from investors, regulators, and even board members.

The bull market of the 1990s provided the perfect environment for Enron's aggressive growth strategy, as investors rewarded companies that demonstrated rapid revenue and earnings expansion regardless of the underlying sustainability of their business models. The dot-com boom created a cultural environment where traditional business metrics like cash flow and asset backing seemed less important than vision, growth potential, and market positioning. Enron capitalized on this environment by presenting itself as a "new economy" company that happened to operate in the energy sector, rather than a traditional energy company that used new technologies.

EnronOnline, launched in November 1999, exemplified this positioning and represented both the pinnacle of Skilling's vision and the beginning of Enron's most dangerous period. The online trading platform allowed real-time trading of energy contracts and positioned Enron as a technology leader rather than a traditional commodity trader. By 2001, EnronOnline was executing trades worth approximately $2.5 billion per day, making it one of the world's largest e-commerce platforms. However, the platform also enabled increasingly speculative trading and complex financial engineering that would later contribute to the company's collapse.

The diversification strategy that Enron pursued during the late 1990s reflected both ambitious growth targets and a concerning detachment from core competencies. The company expanded into electricity trading, broadband services, water utilities, and even weather derivatives, creating a portfolio of businesses that shared little beyond Skilling's belief that "anything that can be traded will be traded". This diversification strategy, while potentially innovative, also dispersed management attention and created operational complexities that strained the organization's ability to maintain adequate risk controls and oversight.

From a systems theory perspective, Enron's rapid growth and diversification created what complexity scientists call "emergent complexity"—a situation where simple rules and strategies produce unpredictably complex organizational behaviors that exceed any individual's ability to understand or control. The company's web of subsidiaries, partnerships, and trading relationships became so intricate that even senior executives struggled to understand the full scope of the organization's activities and exposures. This complexity was not accidental but strategic, as it enabled aggressive accounting practices and regulatory arbitrage while making detection and oversight extremely difficult.

The risk management infrastructure that Enron developed during this period exemplified the company's paradoxical relationship with both innovation and control. The Risk Assessment and Control (RAC) group that oversaw trading activities was staffed by highly qualified professionals who used sophisticated mathematical models to evaluate potential exposures. However, the group's effectiveness was undermined by the same cultural pressures that affected the rest of the organization. RAC analysts knew that rejecting profitable deals could result in retaliation during performance reviews, creating strong incentives to approve questionable transactions.

The compensation structure that Skilling implemented aligned employee incentives with short-term financial results in ways that would later prove catastrophic. Stock options and bonuses tied to quarterly earnings and stock price performance created powerful motivations to manipulate financial results, especially as the company's underlying business performance began to deteriorate. These incentive structures reflected broader trends in executive compensation during the 1990s but were implemented at Enron with unusual intensity and limited oversight.

As Enron entered the new millennium, the company had succeeded in transforming itself from a regional pipeline operator into a global energy trading giant with a market capitalization exceeding $70 billion. The transformation represented a genuine business innovation that created substantial value for customers, employees, and initially for shareholders. However, the same cultural and organizational characteristics that enabled this transformation—aggressive risk-taking, competitive intensity, financial complexity, and limited oversight—also created the conditions that would enable massive fraud and ultimately lead to the company's destruction.

The philosophical and anthropological lessons of Enron's origins and early growth are profound and enduring. The company's story demonstrates how human cognitive limitations, evolutionary psychological tendencies, and modern organizational structures can interact in dangerous ways. Skilling's vision of intellectual meritocracy and market-driven efficiency reflected genuine insights about the potential benefits of applying analytical rigor to traditional industries, but it also created a culture that was vulnerable to the very biases and limitations that careful analysis should help overcome. The rank-and-yank system that was intended to promote excellence instead fostered the tribalism and competitive pressures that enabled collective self-deception and ethical compromise.

The origins of Enron also illustrate the complex relationship between innovation and regulation in modern capitalism. Lay and Skilling's ability to capitalize on deregulation created genuine benefits for energy markets and consumers, but it also exposed the limitations of regulatory frameworks designed for simpler, more transparent business models. The company's rapid growth and increasing complexity outpaced the ability of regulators, auditors, and even its own board of directors to maintain effective oversight, creating the governance vacuum that would later be filled by fraudulent practices.

Understanding Enron's origins and early growth is essential for comprehending both the specific mechanisms that enabled its fraud and the broader systemic vulnerabilities that continue to characterize modern corporate capitalism. The company's transformation from pipeline operator to trading powerhouse demonstrates both the creative potential and destructive risks of financial innovation, while its cultural evolution under Skilling's leadership reveals the psychological and social dynamics that can enable collec

# Chapter Three
## *Key Players and Their Roles*

The Enron scandal was not a product of faceless corporate machinations, but of identifiable people—leaders, architects, accomplices, dissenters, and regulators. Examining these key players and their roles illuminates the confluence of character, cognitive bias, organizational incentives, and institutional failure and reveals how collective and individual decisions intersect to create systemic catastrophe. Enron's story thus invites interdisciplinary scrutiny: how philosophical, psychological, legal, and organizational factors conditioned the behavior and fate of its principal agents.

**Kenneth Lay: Leadership and Ethical Ambiguities**

Kenneth Lay's rise—from modest Midwestern roots and a Ph.D. in economics to Enron's founder and chairman—was fueled by personal ambition, charisma, and an ardent faith in the transformative power of market deregulation. Lay's leadership style embodied the paradoxes at the heart of Enron's success and failure. Publicly championing corporate responsibility and philanthropy, Lay cultivated an image of an ethical steward—Enron's "father figure." Privately, his ambiguous approach to ethical and legal boundaries permitted and sometimes encouraged the aggressive risk-taking, financial maneuvering, and obfuscation that would later be exposed as fraudulent.

Lay's belief in deregulation was both visionary and dangerous. While he ably steered Enron through the transition from a regional pipeline company to a trading innovator, he also presided over the creation of a corporate environment where pressure for performance and profit outpaced institutional checks—where rules became "flexible" and ethical commands were subordinated to the practical logic of market supremacy. Lay's ambiguity was crystallized when faced with mounting signs of fraud in 2001: instead of initiating urgent reform, he publicly reassured stakeholders, selling stock and repeating Enron's aspirational narrative while the company unraveled beneath the surface. Whether Lay was culpably negligent or cynically complicit remains debated, but his failure to impose decisive and accountable leadership in crisis was central to Enron's collapse.

**Jeffrey Skilling: Vision, Aggression, and Complicity in Fraud**

Jeffrey Skilling, Enron's CEO and apostle of market transformation, brought academic brilliance and a gambler's instincts to the company. His "Gas Bank" model, which made energy a globally traded commodity, opened vast opportunities for innovation—and for ever more abstract, opaque business models. Skilling's embrace of mark-to-market accounting and financial engineering enabled Enron to book speculative future profits as tangible earnings, making stock price the barometer of success and fueling an obsession with quarterly targets.

Skilling's management philosophy extolled the intellectual "best and brightest" and famously instituted the "rank and yank" performance system, creating constant anxiety and competition. This system entrenched a culture of hyper-competition, where loyalty to aggressive targets trumped loyalty to ethical standards or holistic thinking. Skilling's disdain for external scrutiny and preference for complexity veiled growing risks. As losses mounted, Skilling was complicit in authorizing off-balance-sheet vehicles and structured transactions that concealed Enron's debt and inflated performance. His abrupt resignation in August 2001, mere months before bankruptcy, shielded him from immediate repercussions but later exposed him to indictment and conviction for multiple counts of fraud.

**Andrew Fastow: Architect of the Special Purpose Entities**

Chief Financial Officer Andrew Fastow was the master engineer of Enron's shadow financial empire. Fastow's creation and management of Special Purpose Entities (SPEs)—entities like LJM, Chewco, and RADR—permitted Enron to move debt off its balance sheet, hide risk, and present a facade of growth and vitality to investors and analysts. Fastow's innovation exploited the fine line between legal financial structuring and outright fraud. Crucially, he and his associates often managed or held stakes in these same SPEs, generating personal profits that represented clear conflicts of interest and violated both fiduciary duty and Enron's code of conduct.

Fastow's conduct epitomized the dangers of unrestrained executive autonomy and weak oversight. He repeatedly assured the board and auditors of the legitimacy of his transactions, while actively concealing their true nature. Federal indictments and subsequent convictions documented how Fastow, through side deals, kickbacks, and complex partnerships, siphoned financial gains for himself and his circle, at enormous cost to shareholders and employees.

## Other Executives, Legal and Accounting Firms: The Role of Arthur Andersen

Enron's leadership was complemented by a cadre of senior executives who executed and perpetuated its strategic and ethical misadventures. Richard Causey, Chief Accounting Officer; Michael Kopper, a Fastow lieutenant; and others within the financial operations enabled, justified, and extended the fraudulent structures than ran through Enron's books. External law firms, most notably Vinson & Elkins, provided opinions that insulated questionable transactions from true scrutiny, helping to sustain the corporate narrative and protect leadership from challenges.

The company's relationship with Arthur Andersen, Enron's auditor, is a case study in the failure of professional gatekeeping. Andersen received as much or more money from consultancy and non-audit services as from actual auditing—creating deep conflicts of interest. Despite repeated questions and warnings—including from whistleblowers inside Andersen itself—the audit partner assigned to Enron continued to sign off on questionable transactions and financial statements. Andersen's eventual destruction of documents and subsequent criminal conviction for obstruction of justice highlighted the extent to which professional service firms' self-interest and compromised independence can erode the ethical infrastructure of financial capitalism.

## Whistleblowers and Internal Dissent

No account of Enron's saga is complete without recognition of those who sought to call attention to malpractice from within—a group ultimately branded "whistleblowers." Most prominent was Sherron Watkins, a vice president in finance, who wrote a detailed memo to Kenneth Lay warning of "an implosion waiting to happen." Watkins and others faced rebuff, internal exile, and threats to their livelihoods for spotlighting fraud. These reactions highlight a culture of silencing and intimidation, pervasive not only within Enron but in much of American business life, where dissenters are often marginalized and retaliation can be severe.

Academic research and post-Enron legislation have emphasized the vital systemic role of whistleblowers and the conditions necessary for their protection. After Enron, the Sarbanes-Oxley Act imposed new responsibilities on boards and executives for the receipt and investigation of internal controls and protected employees who report fraud or violations. The Enron case, however, remains a cautionary tale about how power asymmetries, tribal loyalty, and the pursuit of personal and institutional success can collectively mute principled resistance.

## Conclusion

The key players in Enron's scandal did not act in a vacuum. Their decisions were shaped by a culture of performativity, the architecture of incentives and oversight, the complexity of law and finance, and enduring features of human psychology: loyalty, ambition, competitive tribalism, and rationalization. Their stories speak to both systemic failure and the moral dilemmas faced by individuals navigating high-stakes organizational life. Only through an interdisciplinary lens—philosophical, legal, cognitive, and historical—can the lessons of Enron's "characters" be fully grasped, providing enduring value for theorists, practitioners, and the broader public.

# Chapter Four
## The Mechanics of Fraud and Deception

Understanding the specific mechanisms through which Enron perpetrated its massive fraud requires examining the intersection of accounting technicalities, human psychology, regulatory gaps, and organizational incentives. The company's deceptive practices were not simple acts of embezzlement or straightforward financial theft, but rather sophisticated manipulations of accounting rules, financial instruments, and corporate structures that exploited both systemic vulnerabilities and cognitive biases. From a philosophical anthropological perspective, these mechanisms reveal how modern financial systems can be weaponized by individuals who understand how to exploit the gap between technical compliance and substantive honesty—a gap that exists precisely because human cognitive architecture evolved for small-group interactions where reputation and reciprocity provided natural constraints on deceptive behavior.

## Complex Accounting Practices: Mark-to-Market and Off-Balance-Sheet Entities

The foundation of Enron's fraudulent empire rested on the aggressive exploitation of mark-to-market (MTM) accounting, a legitimate financial practice that became a tool for systematic deception when applied beyond its intended scope. Mark-to-market accounting allows companies to record the current market value of assets and liabilities on their balance sheets, rather than their historical cost. For actively traded securities with transparent market prices, this approach provides more accurate financial information. However, Enron extended MTM accounting to long-term energy contracts—some lasting up to twenty years—where no active markets existed and future values were highly speculative.

Jeffrey Skilling's successful petition to the Securities and Exchange Commission in 1992 to use mark-to-market accounting for Enron's energy trading operations represented a pivotal moment that would enable massive future fraud. Under this method, Enron could immediately book the present value of estimated future profits from energy contracts, regardless of whether those profits would ever materialize. The company's analysts would project cash flows decades into the future, discount them to present value using optimistic assumptions, and record the resulting figures as current earnings. This practice transformed Enron from a company that earned money by delivering energy services into one that created apparent profits through financial projections and accounting manipulations.

The psychological and cognitive dimensions of this practice are profound. Mark-to-market accounting exploited what behavioral economists call "optimism bias"—the human tendency to overestimate the likelihood of positive outcomes while underestimating risks. Enron's executives and analysts, under intense pressure to meet quarterly earnings targets, consistently made rosy projections about future energy prices, contract performance, and market conditions. These optimistic assumptions were not necessarily conscious deceptions initially, but reflected the natural human tendency to believe that current success will continue indefinitely—a cognitive pattern that served early humans well in stable environments but becomes dangerous in complex, rapidly changing markets.

Off-balance-sheet accounting through Special Purpose Entities (SPEs) represented an even more sophisticated form of financial manipulation that exploited both regulatory loopholes and human cognitive limitations. SPEs are legally separate entities that can be used for legitimate purposes such as isolating specific business risks or facilitating complex financial transactions. However, Enron systematically abused these structures to hide debt, inflate revenue, and create the appearance of financial health while the company deteriorated.

The technical requirements for off-balance-sheet treatment under Generally Accepted Accounting Principles (GAAP) required that external investors contribute at least 3 percent of an SPE's capital, with the remaining 97 percent potentially coming from the sponsoring company. This seemingly minor technical requirement created enormous opportunities for manipulation, as companies could maintain effective control over SPEs while avoiding consolidation on their financial statements. Enron exploited this loophole by creating hundreds of SPEs with minimal external investment, often from company employees or affiliated parties who had little real economic interest in the entities' performance.

Special Purpose Entities and Hiding Liabilities

Andrew Fastow's creation and management of SPEs like LJM, LJM2, Chewco, and the Raptor entities represented the apex of Enron's fraudulent financial engineering. These partnerships served multiple deceptive purposes: they moved billions of dollars in debt off Enron's balance sheet, created artificial revenue through sham transactions, and generated personal profits for Fastow and his associates through undisclosed side agreements. The complexity of these structures was not accidental but strategic, designed to confuse auditors, analysts, and regulators while providing legal cover for what were essentially fraudulent transactions.

The LJM partnerships exemplified this strategy. Ostensibly independent investment vehicles managed by Fastow, these entities purchased assets from Enron at inflated prices, immediately improving Enron's quarterly results. However, the partnerships were capitalized primarily with Enron stock and guarantees, meaning that Enron was essentially buying assets from itself using its own stock as payment. When Enron's stock price declined, these arrangements created enormous hidden liabilities that would eventually contribute to the company's bankruptcy.

The Raptor entities presented an even more egregious example of financial manipulation. These SPEs were created ostensibly to hedge Enron's merchant investments—positions in other companies that carried significant market risk. However, the Raptors were capitalized primarily with Enron stock, meaning that they could only provide effective hedging as long as Enron's stock price remained high. When the stock declined, the Raptors lost their ability to cover Enron's losses, creating a deadly spiral where declining stock prices eliminated the company's hedge protection precisely when it was most needed.

From a systems theory perspective, these SPE structures created what complexity scientists call "tight coupling"—a situation where failures in one part of a system rapidly cascade to other parts. The interconnected web of SPEs, all ultimately dependent on Enron's stock price and creditworthiness, meant that any significant decline in the company's market value would trigger simultaneous failures across multiple entities. This tight coupling was hidden from investors and regulators, who viewed the SPEs as independent risk-mitigation tools rather than sources of concentrated systemic risk.

**Round-Trip Trades and Fake Revenue Recognition**

Round-trip trading, also known as "wash trading" or "round-tripping," represented another sophisticated method for inflating Enron's apparent business activity and revenue. These transactions involved simultaneously buying and selling energy commodities at identical prices, creating no net economic value but generating artificial trading volume and revenue that could be reported on financial statements. While the net profit from these transactions was zero, accounting rules allowed companies to report the gross value of both sides of the trade, dramatically inflating apparent revenue.

Enron pioneered and systematized round-trip trading in the energy industry, engaging in these sham transactions with companies like CMS Energy, Reliant Energy, and Dynegy. The practice became so widespread that it created an industry-wide distortion of revenue figures, with energy trading companies reporting revenues that were often ten times larger than their actual net income. This inflation of revenue figures served multiple purposes: it made companies appear larger and more active than they actually were, helped meet Wall

Street growth expectations, and justified high stock valuations based on revenue multiples rather than profitability.

The psychological appeal of round-trip trading lay in its apparent technical legitimacy. These were real contracts involving actual delivery of energy commodities, executed through established trading platforms with proper documentation. From a narrow legal perspective, the trades often complied with the letter of accounting rules while violating their spirit. This allowed executives to engage in deceptive practices while maintaining plausible deniability—they were following established accounting principles, even if those principles were being used to mislead investors.

The merchant model of revenue recognition that Enron adopted represented a related but distinct form of financial manipulation. While traditional energy companies acting as agents reported only their commissions or spreads as revenue, Enron elected to report the full value of energy transactions—both purchases and sales—as gross revenue. This accounting choice, while technically permissible under certain circumstances, dramatically inflated Enron's apparent size and growth rate. Combined with round-trip trading, the merchant model allowed Enron to report revenues of over $100 billion in 2000, when its actual economic value-added was a fraction of that amount.

**Conflicts of Interest and Executive Incentives**

The pervasive conflicts of interest within Enron's executive ranks created a toxic environment where personal enrichment took precedence over fiduciary duty and corporate responsibility. Andrew Fastow's dual role as Enron's CFO and manager of external partnerships represented the most egregious example, but similar conflicts existed throughout the organization. These arrangements violated fundamental principles of corporate governance while enriching executives at shareholders' expense.

Fastow's management of the LJM partnerships while serving as Enron's CFO created an impossible situation where he was essentially negotiating with himself on behalf of different parties. In his role as CFO, Fastow had a fiduciary duty to maximize value for Enron shareholders. As manager of the LJM partnerships, he had a contractual obligation to maximize returns for LJM investors. These competing loyalties inevitably led to transactions that benefited Fastow personally while harming Enron shareholders, particularly as the company's financial condition deteriorated.

The compensation structures within Enron amplified these conflicts by tying executive pay to short-term stock performance and accounting earnings rather than long-term business fundamentals. Stock options, which comprised the majority of senior executive compensation, created powerful incentives to manipulate earnings and maintain artificial stock prices, regardless of underlying business performance. This misalignment between executive incentives and shareholder interests is a classic example of what economists call "agency problems"—situations where agents (executives) pursue their own interests at the expense of principals (shareholders).

Enron's "rank and yank" performance management system further exacerbated these problems by creating intense internal competition and short-term thinking throughout the organization. Employees knew that their continued employment depended on meeting aggressive performance targets, creating powerful incentives to engage in risky or deceptive practices rather than acknowledge problems or underperformance. This system eliminated internal checks and balances, as employees who raised concerns about questionable practices risked being labeled as poor performers and terminated.

**Analyst Complicity and Stock Market Inflation**

The role of Wall Street analysts in enabling and perpetuating Enron's fraud reveals the broader systemic vulnerabilities within the financial markets during the 1990s and early 2000s. Securities analysts, who were supposed to provide independent assessment of public companies' financial prospects, instead became active participants in maintaining Enron's inflated stock price through persistently optimistic recommendations and failure to challenge the company's increasingly complex and opaque business model.

The conflicts of interest within investment banks created powerful incentives for analysts to maintain positive ratings on companies like Enron, regardless of underlying fundamentals. Investment banks earned substantial fees from underwriting Enron's debt and equity offerings, providing advisory services for mergers and acquisitions, and facilitating complex derivative transactions. Analysts who issued negative reports risked losing this lucrative business, creating institutional pressure to maintain favorable coverage even when financial fundamentals deteriorated.

Enron's management actively cultivated relationships with analysts and investors through aggressive investor relations efforts that combined technical complexity with charismatic presentation. Jeffrey Skilling and other executives regularly appeared at investment conferences, analyst meetings, and earnings calls, presenting Enron's business model as revolutionary and transformative while deflecting detailed questions about specific financial arrangements. The company's ability to consistently meet or exceed quarterly earnings expectations—achieved through accounting manipulations—reinforced analyst confidence and justified continued buy recommendations.

The psychological dynamics of analyst behavior reflected broader patterns of group conformity and cognitive bias that anthropologists observe across cultures. Once a consensus formed around Enron's investment attractiveness, individual analysts faced enormous pressure to conform to group opinion. Challenging the prevailing view required not only analytical sophistication but also social courage—the willingness to risk professional relationships and career advancement by contradicting established wisdom. This social pressure was particularly intense in the highly competitive and relationship-driven culture of Wall Street, where contrarian views could lead to professional isolation.

The market inflation that resulted from analyst complicity created a dangerous feedback loop that accelerated Enron's ultimate collapse. High stock prices enabled the company to use its shares as currency for acquisitions, collateral for SPE transactions, and backing for employee compensation. As long as the stock price remained elevated, many of Enron's financial arrangements appeared sustainable. However, when questions about the company's business model finally emerged and the stock began declining, these same arrangements became sources of devastating losses that accelerated the downward spiral.

**Regulatory Arbitrage and Systemic Exploitation**

Enron's fraudulent practices succeeded in part because they exploited gaps and inconsistencies within the regulatory framework governing corporate financial reporting. The company's executives and advisors possessed sophisticated understanding of accounting rules, securities regulations, and tax law, which they used to structure transactions that achieved desired financial statement effects while maintaining technical compliance with legal requirements. This practice, known as "regulatory arbitrage," reveals fundamental weaknesses in rule-based systems that can be gamed by sufficiently motivated and knowledgeable actors.

The international dimension of Enron's operations provided additional opportunities for regulatory arbitrage through jurisdiction shopping and transfer pricing manipulation. The company created hundreds of subsidiaries in offshore jurisdictions with favorable tax and regulatory environments, often for the primary purpose of avoiding U.S. oversight and taxation. These structures made it extremely difficult for any single regulator to understand the company's complete financial picture, creating regulatory blind spots that enabled fraudulent practices.

The evolution of derivatives markets during the 1990s outpaced regulatory frameworks, creating additional opportunities for financial manipulation. Enron pioneered the use of complex derivative instruments in energy markets, often creating new types of contracts that had no established accounting treatment or regulatory oversight. This innovation, while potentially valuable for risk management, also provided cover for transactions designed primarily to achieve desired accounting effects rather than genuine business purposes.

## Conclusion: The Anatomy of Systemic Deception

The mechanics of Enron's fraud reveal how sophisticated financial techniques, cognitive biases, organizational incentives, and regulatory gaps can combine to create opportunities for massive deception. The company's fraudulent practices were not simply violations of accounting rules, but systematic exploitations of vulnerabilities within modern financial systems. Mark-to-market accounting became a tool for transforming speculation into apparent certainty. SPEs enabled the hiding of liabilities and creation of artificial revenues. Round-trip trading inflated business activity and revenue figures. Executive compensation structures created incentives for short-term manipulation over long-term value creation. Analyst conflicts of interest eliminated independent oversight. Regulatory arbitrage exploited gaps in oversight frameworks.

From an interdisciplinary perspective, these mechanisms reflect broader tensions between human psychological tendencies and the requirements of modern financial systems. The cognitive patterns that served early humans well in small-group environments—optimism, tribalism, deference to authority, preference for simple narratives—became liabilities in complex financial markets where success required careful risk assessment, independent judgment, and tolerance for uncertainty. Enron's fraud succeeded by exploiting these cognitive limitations while using technical complexity to defeat oversight mechanisms.

The lasting significance of understanding these mechanics lies not in their historical specificity, but in their revelation of ongoing vulnerabilities within financial markets and corporate governance systems. The same cognitive biases, incentive misalignments, and regulatory gaps that enabled Enron's fraud continue to exist in different forms, creating ongoing risks for investors, employees, and society. Only through careful attention to both technical details and human factors can these vulnerabilities be addressed and future scandals prevented.

# Chapter Five
## Agency Behavior and Corporate Corruption

The Enron scandal provides a textbook illustration of how principal-agent theory explains corporate corruption and the systematic breakdown of fiduciary relationships within modern corporations. At its core, the scandal emerged from a fundamental misalignment between the interests of Enron's executives (agents) and its shareholders, employees, and stakeholders (principals), exacerbated by information asymmetries, perverse incentive structures, and the erosion of monitoring mechanisms that are supposed to protect principals from agent opportunism. From a philosophical anthropological perspective, these agency failures reflect deeper tensions between evolved human psychology—which prioritizes immediate rewards, tribal loyalty, and status competition—and the requirements of modern corporate governance systems that depend on abstract fiduciary duties and long-term thinking.

**Principal-Agent Theory and Conflicts of Interest at Enron**

Principal-agent theory, developed in economics and organizational behavior, describes the relationship between principals (owners or shareholders) who delegate authority to agents (managers and executives) to act on their behalf. The theory predicts that conflicts will inevitably arise because agents and principals have different risk preferences, time horizons, and access to information. Principals, who can diversify their investments across multiple companies, may be relatively risk-neutral and focused on long-term value creation. Agents, whose careers and compensation are tied to a single organization, tend to be risk-averse regarding their employment security while potentially risk-seeking regarding corporate strategies that might enhance their personal compensation.

Enron's corporate structure created particularly severe agency problems due to the complexity of its business model, the opacity of its financial reporting, and the concentration of decision-making power in a small group of executives. The company's transformation from a traditional pipeline operator to a sophisticated trading and financial services firm created information asymmetries that were difficult for outside shareholders to monitor effectively. Jeffrey Skilling's intellectual arrogance and Andrew Fastow's financial engineering expertise created a knowledge gap that the board of directors and external auditors struggled to bridge, enabling increasingly aggressive and ultimately fraudulent practices.

The compensation structure at Enron dramatically amplified these agency problems by creating powerful incentives for short-term manipulation over long-term value creation. Executive compensation was heavily weighted toward stock options and performance bonuses tied to quarterly earnings and stock price appreciation. This structure, while intended to align management interests with shareholder value, actually created perverse incentives for earnings management, accounting manipulation, and excessive risk-taking. Skilling received $132 million in total compensation in 2000, most of it in stock options that would only retain value if Enron's stock price continued rising. This created enormous pressure to maintain the appearance of growth and profitability regardless of underlying business fundamentals.

From a cognitive science perspective, these compensation structures exploited fundamental limitations in human temporal reasoning and risk assessment. Behavioral economists have documented how individuals systematically overweight immediate rewards relative to future costs—a cognitive bias known as "temporal discounting" that served early humans well in environments where immediate survival took precedence over long-term planning. In corporate settings, this bias encourages focus on quarterly earnings and stock price movements rather than sustainable business development, creating vulnerability to the accounting manipulations that characterized Enron's fraud.

**Collusion, Related-Party Transactions, and Insider Trading**

The web of collusion that emerged within Enron's executive ranks represents one of the most systematic examples of agent conspiracy against principal interests in corporate history. Andrew Fastow's creation and management of Special Purpose Entities (SPEs) while serving as Enron's Chief Financial Officer created impossible conflicts of interest that violated fundamental principles of fiduciary duty. As CFO, Fastow owed undivided loyalty to Enron shareholders; as manager of the LJM partnerships, he had contractual obligations to maximize returns for external investors. These competing loyalties inevitably led to transactions that enriched Fastow personally while transferring wealth from Enron shareholders to the partnerships he controlled.

The related-party transactions between Enron and Fastow's SPEs violated both legal requirements for arm's-length dealing and fundamental economic principles of fair market pricing. These transactions were structured to appear as legitimate business arrangements while actually serving to manipulate Enron's financial statements and generate personal profits for company insiders. The LJM partnerships purchased assets from Enron at inflated prices, immediately improving Enron's quarterly earnings while creating hidden liabilities that would later contribute to the company's bankruptcy. Federal prosecutors documented how Fastow earned approximately $45 million from these arrangements, money that effectively represented transfers from Enron shareholders to company executives.

The collusion extended beyond Fastow to include other senior executives, external advisors, and supposedly independent parties. Michael Kopper, Fastow's protégé, managed many of the SPE transactions and received substantial undisclosed compensation. External law firms, particularly Vinson & Elkins, provided legal opinions that legitimized questionable transactions without adequate independent analysis. Banks like Merrill Lynch participated in sham transactions, such as the Nigerian barge deals, that were structured to appear as asset sales while actually functioning as disguised loans.

Insider trading represented another dimension of the agency corruption at Enron, as executives sold large quantities of stock while publicly reassuring investors about the company's financial health. Kenneth Lay sold over $100 million worth of Enron stock in 2000 and 2001 while encouraging employees to increase their holdings in company retirement accounts. Jeffrey Skilling sold $15 million in stock during his final year as CEO while maintaining that Enron's business model was sound and its growth prospects excellent. These sales, while technically legal, represented clear violations of the fiduciary duty to provide accurate information to shareholders and demonstrated how executives prioritized personal financial gain over stakeholder interests.

From an anthropological perspective, this pattern of collusion reflects deeply ingrained human tendencies toward in-group loyalty and reciprocal exchange that can become corrupted in modern organizational contexts. The small group of Enron executives developed what anthropologists would recognize as a "gift economy" where mutual enrichment through questionable transactions created bonds of loyalty that superseded their obligations to external stakeholders. This tribal dynamic, which serves important social functions in small-scale societies, became pathological when applied to modern corporations where fiduciary duties are supposed to override personal relationships.

**Organizational Ethics, Control Failures, and Cultural Enabling**

The systematic failure of ethical oversight within Enron reveals how organizational culture, control systems, and leadership behavior interact to either prevent or enable corporate corruption. Enron's corporate culture, shaped by Jeffrey Skilling's intellectual arrogance and competitive intensity, created an environment where ethical considerations were subordinated to financial performance and where dissent was discouraged through formal and informal sanctions. The company's "rank and yank" performance management system eliminated employees who failed to meet aggressive targets, creating powerful incentives to achieve results regardless of means.

The board of directors failed in its fundamental duty to provide independent oversight of management decisions and risk management practices. Despite being comprised of respected business leaders and academics, the board consistently deferred to management assertions about complex financial transactions and failed to ask probing questions about the company's increasingly opaque business model. The Powers Report, commissioned by Enron's board after the scandal emerged, documented how directors routinely approved related-party transactions without adequate independent analysis, relying instead on management representations and perfunctory legal opinions.

Internal control systems that were supposed to prevent fraud and ensure accurate financial reporting were systematically undermined by the same cultural and incentive problems that affected other aspects of the organization. The Risk Assessment and Control (RAC) group, responsible for evaluating trading risks, faced enormous pressure to approve profitable transactions even when they involved questionable accounting or excessive risk exposure. Employees knew that challenging management decisions could result in poor performance reviews and termination, creating strong incentives to acquiesce to questionable practices.

Arthur Andersen's failure as an external control mechanism illustrates how conflicts of interest and cultural pressures can corrupt supposedly independent oversight institutions. Andersen received substantial consulting fees from Enron in addition to audit fees, creating financial incentives to maintain positive relationships with management rather than provide independent oversight. The accounting firm's Houston office, which managed the Enron relationship, developed a culture of deference to client management that overrode professional skepticism and audit standards.

The phenomenon of "ethical fading" explains how initially well-intentioned individuals gradually compromised their moral standards through a series of small steps that seemed individually justifiable. Enron executives didn't suddenly decide to commit massive fraud; instead, they made incremental decisions to bend accounting rules, hide information from auditors, and prioritize short-term results over long-term sustainability. Each compromise made subsequent violations easier to rationalize, creating a downward spiral of ethical deterioration that culminated in systematic fraud.

From a neuroscientific perspective, the high-pressure, competitive environment at Enron created conditions that impaired ethical decision-making by triggering stress responses that override the prefrontal cortex's capacity for careful moral reasoning. Chronic stress and time pressure activate the limbic system's fight-or-flight responses while suppressing the brain regions responsible for long-term planning and ethical reflection. This neurological response, adaptive for immediate physical threats, becomes maladaptive in complex organizational environments where ethical reasoning is essential for sustainable performance.

## Systemic Enablers and Regulatory Capture

The agency corruption at Enron was enabled by broader systemic failures in regulatory oversight, professional standards, and market mechanisms that were supposed to detect and prevent corporate fraud. The Securities and Exchange Commission's limited resources and expertise made it difficult to monitor complex financial instruments and business models that exceeded traditional regulatory frameworks. The Financial Accounting Standards Board's rules governing SPEs and off-balance-sheet financing provided loopholes that sophisticated financial engineers could exploit while maintaining technical compliance with accounting standards.

Credit rating agencies, which were supposed to provide independent assessment of corporate creditworthiness, failed to detect or adequately disclose the risks embedded in Enron's complex financial structure. Standard & Poor's, Moody's, and Fitch maintained investment-grade ratings on Enron debt until shortly before the company's bankruptcy, despite clear evidence of financial distress and accounting irregularities. These agencies faced their own conflicts of interest, as they were paid by the companies they rated and competed for business by providing favorable assessments.

The financial press and securities analysts, who were supposed to provide independent scrutiny of corporate performance, instead became cheerleaders for Enron's growth story. The complexity of Enron's business model and the company's aggressive investor relations efforts created information asymmetries that made independent analysis difficult. Analysts who asked probing questions about specific transactions or accounting practices were often dismissed as failing to understand Enron's innovative business model.

Investment banks played a crucial enabling role by creating and marketing the complex financial instruments that Enron used to manipulate its financial statements. Banks like JPMorgan Chase, Citigroup, and Credit Suisse First Boston structured transactions that had no legitimate business purpose beyond achieving desired accounting treatment. These institutions earned substantial fees from these arrangements while maintaining plausible deniability about their ultimate purpose.

## Psychological and Anthropological Dimensions of Corporate Corruption

The psychological mechanisms that enabled corruption at Enron reflect universal human tendencies that become problematic in modern organizational contexts. Cognitive dissonance theory explains how individuals reduce psychological tension between their actions and their moral beliefs by rationalizing unethical behavior. Enron executives convinced themselves that aggressive accounting practices were necessary innovations that created value for stakeholders, even as these practices violated fundamental principles of financial transparency and fiduciary duty.

Social identity theory illuminates how group membership and loyalty can override individual moral judgment. Enron's executives developed strong in-group identification that made them view external critics as threats to be defeated rather than legitimate voices raising important concerns. This tribal mentality, reinforced by financial success and media attention, created a collective sense of superiority that insulated the group from external feedback and internal dissent.

The concept of "moral disengagement," developed by psychologist Albert Bandura, explains how individuals can behave unethically while maintaining their sense of moral identity through psychological mechanisms such as euphemistic labeling, advantageous comparison, and diffusion of responsibility. Enron executives described fraud as "aggressive accounting," compared their practices favorably to competitors' behavior, and blamed external pressures for forcing them to manipulate financial results.

**Implications for Corporate Governance and Regulation**

The agency failures at Enron have profound implications for understanding the limitations of current corporate governance systems and the need for structural reforms that address both technical and psychological vulnerabilities. Traditional approaches that rely primarily on monitoring and punishment may be insufficient to address the complex psychological and social dynamics that enable corporate corruption. More effective approaches must address the cultural, incentive, and organizational factors that shape individual and group behavior within corporations.

The Sarbanes-Oxley Act of 2002, passed in response to Enron and other corporate scandals, represents an important step toward addressing some of these vulnerabilities through enhanced disclosure requirements, executive certification of financial statements, and stronger penalties for corporate fraud. However, the law's emphasis on compliance and control may be insufficient to address the cultural and psychological factors that enable corruption. Research suggests that values-based approaches that emphasize ethical leadership, cultural transformation, and intrinsic motivation may be more effective than purely rule-based systems.

## Conclusion

The agency behavior and corporate corruption at Enron represents a failure of multiple systems—governance, oversight, regulation, and culture—that were supposed to align agent behavior with principal interests. The scandal reveals how sophisticated financial techniques, psychological biases, organizational incentives, and regulatory gaps can combine to enable systematic wealth transfers from stakeholders to corporate insiders. Understanding these mechanisms requires an interdisciplinary approach that integrates insights from economics, psychology, anthropology, and organizational behavior to address both the technical and human dimensions of corporate governance.

The lasting significance of Enron's agency failures lies not in their historical specificity but in their revelation of ongoing vulnerabilities within modern capitalism that continue to create opportunities for corruption and fraud. Only through careful attention to both structural reforms and cultural transformation can these vulnerabilities be addressed and similar scandals prevented in the future.

# Chapter Six
## The Systemic Roots of Enron's Collapse

The collapse of Enron is often reduced in popular media to a story of corporate greed and malfeasance. Yet this simplistic portrayal conceals layered structural, ideological, and cognitive dynamics that conspired over decades to enable one of the most infamous corporate frauds in modern history. Enron's spectacular implosion was not merely the outcome of individual failing or rogue actors but a failure rooted deeply in the political economy, regulatory architecture, and cultural norms of late twentieth-century America, requiring us to look beyond courtroom indictments to an intersectional understanding that incorporates historical, legal, cognitive, and philosophical insights.

In the late 1970s and throughout the 1980s, the United States underwent a profound ideological reorientation under the banner of neoliberalism. Advocates championed the belief that free markets, when unshackled from perceived excessive government constraints, would most efficiently allocate resources, stimulate innovation, and generate economic growth. This ideological transformation drew heavily from the work of economists like Milton Friedman, whose advocacy for free-market capitalism and minimal government intervention became foundational to policy reform. Friedman argued that competitive markets naturally self-correct, eliminating the need for extensive regulation that he viewed as inefficient and distortive. In this intellectual and political milieu, President Ronald Reagan's 1981 characterization of government as "the problem" rather than the solution encapsulated a transformative attitude toward the role of the state. This was a decisive departure from the twentieth-century demand for protective regulation, particularly emanating from lessons learned during the Great Depression that gave rise to the New Deal regulatory state and landmark legislation such as the Securities Act of 1933 and the Securities Exchange Act of 1934.

The neoliberal agenda was implemented through concrete policy changes that reshaped entire sectors of the American economy. Earlier deregulation efforts had already begun in industries like trucking and airlines during the Carter administration, demonstrating what proponents claimed were the benefits of increased competition and market efficiency. These successes provided political momentum for more ambitious deregulation projects that would follow in subsequent decades.

Manifesting this ideological shift were signature legislative acts reshaping whole sectors of the economy. The Energy Policy Act of 1992 deregulated wholesale electricity markets, introducing competition where prior regulation had fostered monopolies and public utility frameworks. This act propelled energy commodities like electricity and natural gas into the realm of tradable financial instruments, spawning vast new markets involving derivatives and other complex contracts scarcely understood by regulators or the market at large. The transformation was revolutionary: what had previously been treated as a public service provided by regulated utilities was suddenly opened to speculative trading and financial engineering.

Similarly, the Telecommunications Act of 1996 dismantled long-standing monopolies, opening competition across telecommunications, yet creating fragmented regulatory oversight amid rapid technological innovation. The act sought to encourage the development of new technologies and services by eliminating barriers between different types of communication companies. While it succeeded in spurring innovation, it also created regulatory confusion as different agencies struggled to coordinate oversight of an increasingly integrated industry.

While these reforms promised consumer benefits and market dynamism, they ushered in uncharted complexity and opacity, testing the limits of existing institutional frameworks. Enron emerged as a prime beneficiary, pioneering complex financial engineering and risk management practices whose opacity masked true financial health beneath layers of special purpose entities and mark-to-market accounting. Through aggressive innovation, Enron exploited regulatory lacunae carved out by deregulation while cultivating a narrative of corporate brilliance and invulnerability, fed by complicit analysts and an uncritical media.

To place these transformations in a richer historical frame, one must recall the Gilded Age of the late nineteenth century, when rapid industrial expansion and laissez-faire doctrine birthed giant trusts and monopolies. During this era, corporate titans like John D. Rockefeller of Standard Oil and Andrew Carnegie in steel built vast industrial empires with minimal government oversight. Regulatory initiatives to contain such power were often thwarted in courts defending "freedom of contract" and economic liberty, stifling efforts to control corporate excess and prompting widespread public disenchantment.

The Sherman Antitrust Act of 1890 represented an early attempt to address monopolistic abuses, but its enforcement was inconsistent and often ineffective. Courts frequently interpreted the act narrowly, protecting business combinations under the guise of economic freedom. This pattern persisted until public outcry and economic instability forced more aggressive enforcement. The Panic of 1893, partly attributed to corporate speculation and manipulation, demonstrated the dangers of unregulated markets and concentrated economic power.

This Gilded Age experience culminated in the Progressive Era reforms, which saw the advent of more comprehensive antitrust laws, the establishment of federal regulatory agencies—including the Interstate Commerce Commission and the Federal Trade Commission—and a greater public role in oversight. The Progressive movement recognized that markets required active regulation to function in the public interest and that concentrated corporate power posed threats to democratic governance.

The late twentieth-century deregulation movement, buoyed by neoliberal optimism, represented a cyclical return to reduced regulatory intervention, repeating many mistakes of the past by neglecting lessons on market failures and corporate concentration. The resurgence of deregulation at the end of the twentieth century, fueled by neoliberal ideology, repeated many of these historical errors. A battered post–Great Depression regulatory framework was once again dismantled, and safeguards against corporate excess faded. This cyclical repetition underscores the dangers of ideological absolutism—faith in market self-regulation often suppresses the institutional memory necessary to prevent recurrence of past crises.

Institutional weakening was evident in the Securities and Exchange Commission's diminished capacity. Charged with policing securities markets since 1934, the SEC confronted rampant product innovation and escalating market volumes with inadequate personnel and budget. By the late 1990s, the SEC's enforcement division boasted fewer than 800 staff members—including lawyers and accountants—to oversee trillions in market capitalization alongside increasingly complex derivative products and corporate disclosures, overwhelming regulatory scrutiny. The mathematical reality was stark: each enforcement professional was theoretically responsible for overseeing billions of dollars in market activity, an impossible task given the complexity of modern financial instruments.

Concurrent with these challenges, legislative adjustments like the Private Securities Litigation Reform Act of 1995 effectively barred many legitimate shareholder suits before discovery and shielded forward-looking statements from liability. This diminished critical checks on corporate wrongdoing and emboldened firms to adopt aggressive accounting with lowered scrutiny. The act was intended to reduce frivolous litigation, but its practical effect was to make it much harder for investors to hold corporations accountable for misleading statements or fraudulent behavior.

From a jurisprudential perspective, these failures resonate with Lon Fuller's doctrine of the "inner morality of law," which holds that laws require enforceability to have normative force. Fuller emphasized that law must be clear, consistent, publicly known, and practically enforceable to function as genuine moral guidance. Laws that are impossible or unequally enforced become symbolic rather than practical instruments of justice and order. In Enron's case, statutes and regulations existed but were deprived of operational teeth by resource constraints and political impatience. The regulatory framework had become what Fuller would recognize as a form of "hollow law"—formally present but functionally impotent.

Political theorist Hannah Arendt's insights into authority further illuminate the collapse. Arendt distinguished authority from power or violence, characterizing it as legitimate rule sustained by voluntary acceptance grounded in shared norms. Authority, in Arendt's conception, derives its legitimacy not from force but from recognition of its rightful place in maintaining social order and common values. Enron's leadership commanded a charismatic authority that dissolved critical accountability mechanisms within boards and oversight bodies, which capitulated to deference instead of exercising independent judgment. This dynamic mirrored Arendt's concern that unreflective submission to authority undermines institutional integrity, enabling irresponsibility and ethical decay.

The boards of directors at Enron exemplified this failure of authority. Rather than serving as independent overseers challenging management decisions, board members often deferred to the charismatic leadership of Kenneth Lay and Jeffrey Skilling. This deference was reinforced by social dynamics, financial incentives, and the complexity of Enron's business model, which made independent evaluation difficult.

Karl Popper's insistence on falsifiability and open societal critique complements this framework. Popper warned that closed epistemic systems—communities and institutions intolerant of dissent—breed dogmatism and prevent correction. His philosophy emphasized that healthy institutions must remain open to criticism and revision based on evidence. Enron's milieu, including its regulatory and media echo chambers, exemplified such closure, insulating the myth of success from skepticism until the facade collapsed abruptly. Analysts who dared to question Enron's complex financial structures faced pressure and ostracism from both the company and their peers.

Human cognitive limitations compounded institutional failures. Herbert Simon's theory of bounded rationality illuminates how contextual constraints—imperfect information, limited time, and finite cognitive capacity—force decision-makers, including regulators and auditors, to rely on heuristics and satisficing rather than exhaustive rationality. Simon's work revealed that humans do not make perfectly rational decisions but instead make choices that are "good enough" given their constraints and limitations.

These cognitive shortcuts often resulted in systematic biases such as confirmation bias, anchoring, availability heuristics, and groupthink, dimming the perception of risk and reinforcing complacency within Enron and among its overseers. Confirmation bias led auditors and regulators to seek information that confirmed their existing beliefs about Enron's stability rather than actively looking for contradictory evidence. Anchoring bias caused initial positive impressions to unduly influence subsequent judgments, even when new information suggested problems.

The overconfidence bias prevalent in executive and regulatory circles instilled misplaced certainty in controlling complex financial mechanisms despite evident warning signs. Group dynamics and social pressures further stifled dissenting voices essential to challenging prevailing narratives. Arthur Andersen auditors, for example, were embedded within Enron's culture to such an extent that they lost their independence and ability to provide objective oversight.

Historical precedents reinforce these conclusions. The Savings and Loan crisis of the 1980s paralleled Enron in its deregulation-induced risk-taking, flawed oversight, and bailout of hundreds of billions. Deregulation allowed thrift institutions to dramatically expand beyond traditional home mortgages into riskier commercial real estate and speculative ventures. The result was a wave of insolvencies that required a massive taxpayer-funded bailout exceeding $100 billion.

This crisis laid bare institutional weaknesses in regulatory agencies like the Federal Home Loan Bank Board, which operated with limited oversight tools and faced political interference.

Rating agencies and auditors, then as in the Enron episode, were compromised by conflicts of interest—often serving as consultants to the firms they were supposed to scrutinize, undermining objectivity. This failure of oversight structure, punctuated by cognitive blind spots and regulatory capture, directly foreshadowed later Enron-related collapses. The pattern was consistent: deregulation created opportunities for excessive risk-taking, oversight institutions were weakened or captured, and cognitive biases prevented recognition of accumulating dangers until crisis struck.

Similarly, the 2008 financial crisis unfolded amid opaque derivatives and bundled mortgage securities, instruments designed to spread and hide risks. Like Enron's SPEs, these financial innovations created illusory stability while concentrating systemic risk. Regulatory agencies, overwhelmed by complexity and under-resourced, again failed to interrogate the assumptions behind complex products that they did not fully understand.

Addressing these intertwined failures requires a fundamentally interdisciplinary approach. Legal reform must ensure enforceable normative clarity supported by institutional strength. This means not just writing better laws but ensuring that regulatory agencies have the resources, expertise, and political support necessary to enforce them effectively.

Governance reforms should cultivate cultures valuing critical dissent and diversity of expertise. Corporate boards need members with relevant technical knowledge and the independence to challenge management. Decision-making processes should incorporate awareness training for cognitive vulnerabilities and employ mechanisms such as red teams and pre-mortem risk assessments to identify potential problems before they become crises.

Systems theory reminds us that tightly coupled financial networks require attention to feedback loops and cascading failures. Modern financial systems are so interconnected that problems at one institution can quickly spread throughout the entire system, as the 2008 crisis demonstrated.

Markets, as Karl Polanyi forcefully argued in The Great Transformation, are embedded within social relations and political institutions. They cannot operate effectively or justly when abstracted from the cultural and normative frameworks that enforce ethical behavior and mutual accountability. Polanyi's concept of "embeddedness" suggests that attempts to create purely self-regulating markets inevitably fail because markets are social institutions that depend on shared values, legal frameworks, and cultural norms.

Recognizing markets as socially constructed entities profoundly shapes regulatory design, emphasizing governance and ethical culture over market autonomy and self-policing rhetoric. This perspective challenges the neoliberal assumption that markets can function independently of social and political oversight.

Simon's bounded rationality further grounds this view by highlighting human cognitive limits. Rather than assuming actors calculate optimal decisions, his work encourages us to design institutions that account for heuristic biases and limited information processing, thus improving resilience. This means creating systems with built-in redundancy, multiple perspectives, and mechanisms for error correction.

Popper's epistemology emphasizes the importance of open criticism and falsifiability in healthy institutions. Institutions must be structured to welcome challenges to prevailing assumptions and to change course when evidence contradicts established beliefs. Enron's tragedy was partly shaped by closed institutional cultures resistant to critique, which delayed exposure of damaging practices until the company was beyond salvation.

Fuller's moral theory of law reminds regulators and legislators that rules must be clear, consistently enforced, and congruent with social realities to be effective. Enron's experience shows how legal formalism fails when divorced from practical enforcement and ethical culture. Laws on paper are meaningless without the institutional capacity and political will to implement them.

Arendt's analysis of authority uniquely illuminates the relational dynamics in governance. Legitimate authority draws on communal recognition, which collapses when authority is uncritically accepted in place of active oversight. Enron's leadership exploited charismatic authority to erode institutional checks and balances, substituting personal loyalty for professional accountability.

These intellectual traditions, when integrated, offer a multidimensional diagnosis of Enron's collapse: ideological zeal for deregulation, institutional atrophy, inadequate legal frameworks, cognitive biases, closed epistemic systems, and corrupted authority all interplayed to produce systemic failure. This amplified understanding moves beyond superficial blame to systemic, cultural, and psychological insights requisite for lasting reform.

Contemporary reforms, particularly the Sarbanes-Oxley Act passed in response to Enron and other scandals, represent attempts to address some of these systemic weaknesses. The act strengthened auditing standards, improved corporate disclosure requirements, and increased penalties for financial fraud. However, critics argue that such reforms, while necessary, are insufficient without addressing the deeper cultural and institutional factors that enabled the crisis.

Legacy crises such as the Savings and Loan disaster and the 2008 financial meltdown echo these patterns, underscoring the necessity of resilient designs incorporating ethics, transparency, expertise, and critical inquiry embedded within effective legal structures. Each crisis teaches similar lessons about the dangers of excessive deregulation, the importance of independent oversight, and the need to account for human cognitive limitations in institutional design.

Enron's spectacular demise, then, is more than just a cautionary tale of corporate fraud; it is a stark exposition of modern capitalism's vulnerabilities—rooted in ideology, culture, human nature, and institutional failures—that demand comprehensive, interdisciplinary responses to safeguard democratic economies. The lessons learned must inform not only regulatory reform but also broader questions about the relationship between markets, democracy, and social responsibility in the twenty-first century.

# Chapter Seven
# Internal Corporate Culture and Leadership Failures

The Enron collapse cannot be understood merely as a failure of external oversight or regulatory gaps. At its core, Enron's downfall was a product of profound internal dysfunction—a toxic organizational culture, compromised leadership, and systemic breakdown of corporate governance. These internal failures created an environment where deception flourished, dissent was silenced, and ethical boundaries dissolved in pursuit of short-term financial gains.

The transformation of Enron from a traditional pipeline company into an energy trading powerhouse began with fundamental changes to its organizational DNA. Under the leadership of Kenneth Lay and particularly Jeffrey Skilling, Enron evolved from a conservative utility company with straightforward operations into a hyper-aggressive trading organization that prioritized financial innovation over operational excellence. This metamorphosis was not merely strategic but deeply cultural, reshaping the values, incentives, and behavioral norms that governed employee conduct throughout the organization.

Kenneth Lay's leadership embodied the contradictions that would ultimately define Enron's culture. Publicly championing corporate responsibility and ethical conduct while privately permitting, and sometimes actively encouraging, the aggressive risk-taking and financial maneuvering that would later be exposed as fraudulent. Lay cultivated an image as Enron's "father figure," projecting warmth and moral authority while presiding over an organization that systematically violated the very principles he espoused. His office displayed an Enron paperweight inscribed with "Vision and Values," yet the company's actual practices reflected a profound disconnect between stated ideals and operational reality.

This disconnect was not merely cosmetic but reflected deeper philosophical tensions within Lay's approach to leadership. His unwavering belief in deregulation and market efficiency, while visionary in many respects, created blind spots that prevented him from recognizing the dangerous dynamics emerging within his organization. When confronted with mounting evidence of financial irregularities, Lay's response was to reassure stakeholders and maintain the narrative of success rather than initiate decisive reforms or accountability measures.

Jeffrey Skilling's arrival at Enron in 1990 marked the beginning of a cultural revolution that would fundamentally reshape the company's identity and operational philosophy. Skilling brought with him the intellectual framework and analytical tools he had developed during his tenure as a McKinsey & Company consultant, approaching the energy business through the lens of financial theory rather than operational expertise. His breakthrough insight—transforming Enron from a company that owned physical assets into one that traded energy contracts and managed financial risk—represented genuine innovation but also contained the seeds of the company's eventual destruction.

Skilling's "Gas Bank" concept, developed in the early 1990s, demonstrated both his intellectual capabilities and his preference for abstract financial models over tangible business fundamentals. By buying gas supply contracts from producers and selling them to consumers while managing the associated risks, Enron could generate profits from spreads while providing valuable services to market participants. This business model required sophisticated risk management capabilities and deep understanding of both physical energy markets and financial derivatives—skills that Enron would develop over the following decade but never fully master.

The organizational culture that emerged under Skilling's leadership reflected his background in elite consulting and his belief in intellectual meritocracy. He systematically recruited top graduates from prestigious MBA programs, creating what he termed a culture of the "best and brightest" that valued analytical prowess and competitive intensity above traditional business virtues such as operational excellence, customer service, or ethical conduct. This approach fostered innovation and attracted exceptional talent but also created an environment of intellectual arrogance that dismissed skepticism as evidence of inferior capability.

Skilling's implementation of the "rank and yank" performance management system, borrowed from General Electric's Jack Welch, created an intensely Darwinian environment where employees were rated against each other every six months, with the bottom 15-20 percent facing termination regardless of absolute performance levels. This system was designed to maintain competitive pressure and eliminate complacency, but it also fostered destructive internal competition that undermined collaboration and encouraged short-term thinking at the expense of long-term sustainability.

From a cognitive science perspective, Skilling's management approach created conditions that would later enable Enron's fraudulent practices. High-pressure competitive environments trigger stress responses that impair the prefrontal cortex's ability to engage in careful ethical reasoning while enhancing the limbic system's focus on immediate rewards and threat avoidance. The rank-and-yank system fostered in-group/out-group dynamics that anthropologists recognize as fundamental to human social organization but which become toxic in corporate environments when they override broader organizational or societal values.

The hiring of Andrew Fastow as Chief Financial Officer in 1998 represents one of the most consequential personnel decisions in corporate history. Fastow quickly distinguished himself through his ability to create complex financial structures that appeared to reduce risk while actually concentrating it in hidden and dangerous ways. His rise through Enron's ranks demonstrated both the company's meritocratic culture and its growing emphasis on financial engineering over fundamental business operations.

Fastow's creation and management of Special Purpose Entities (SPEs) such as LJM, LJM2, Chewco, and the Raptor entities represented the apex of Enron's fraudulent financial engineering. These partnerships served multiple deceptive purposes: they moved billions of dollars in debt off Enron's balance sheet, created artificial revenue through sham transactions, and generated personal profits for Fastow and his associates through undisclosed side agreements that represented clear conflicts of interest.

The organizational culture that enabled these practices reflected broader failures of corporate governance and ethical leadership. Enron's emphasis on intellectual capital over physical assets led to increasingly abstract business models that were difficult for outsiders—and even many insiders—to understand or evaluate. This opacity was initially seen as a competitive advantage, making it difficult for competitors to replicate Enron's strategies, but it later became a tool for concealing fraudulent practices from investors, regulators, and board members.

The compensation structure that Skilling implemented aligned employee incentives with short-term financial results in ways that proved catastrophic. Stock options and bonuses tied to quarterly earnings and stock price performance created powerful motivations to manipulate financial results, especially as the company's underlying business performance began to deteriorate. These incentive structures reflected broader trends in executive compensation during the 1990s but were implemented at Enron with unusual intensity and limited oversight.

The risk management infrastructure that Enron developed during its rapid growth exemplified the company's paradoxical relationship with both innovation and control. The Risk Assessment and Control (RAC) group that oversaw trading activities was staffed by highly qualified professionals who used sophisticated mathematical models to evaluate potential exposures. However, the group's effectiveness was undermined by the same cultural pressures that affected the rest of the organization. RAC analysts understood that rejecting profitable deals could result in retaliation during performance reviews, creating strong incentives to approve questionable transactions rather than maintain rigorous risk discipline.

The diversification strategy that Enron pursued during the late 1990s reflected both ambitious growth targets and concerning detachment from core competencies. The company expanded into electricity trading, broadband services, water utilities, and weather derivatives, creating a portfolio of businesses that shared little beyond Skilling's belief that "anything that can be traded will be traded." This diversification strategy dispersed management attention and created operational complexities that strained the organization's ability to maintain adequate risk controls and oversight.

From a systems theory perspective, Enron's rapid growth and diversification created what complexity scientists call "emergent complexity"—a situation where simple rules and strategies produce unpredictably complex organizational behaviors that exceed any individual's ability to understand or control. The company's web of subsidiaries, partnerships, and trading relationships became so intricate that even senior executives struggled to understand the full scope of the organization's activities and exposures.

The board of directors' failure to provide effective oversight represented another critical dimension of Enron's internal governance breakdown. Despite being composed of accomplished individuals with impressive credentials, the board lacked the expertise necessary to understand Enron's increasingly complex business model. Directors were drawn from prestigious universities, law firms, and financial institutions, but few had direct experience in energy trading or structured finance that would have enabled them to evaluate management's strategies effectively.

Board meetings typically featured rapid-fire presentations by charismatic executives who dazzled directors with talk of "new economy" energy markets and innovative financial structures. Few directors possessed the technical knowledge necessary to ask penetrating questions, and the culture of deference that pervaded the boardroom discouraged the kind of skeptical inquiry that effective oversight requires. Fiduciary duty was reduced to ritualistic performance rather than substantive engagement with the company's strategic and operational realities.

The relationship between Enron and its external auditor, Arthur Andersen, exemplified the conflicts of interest that compromised professional oversight. Andersen earned nearly as much from Enron's consulting contracts as from its audit fees, creating structural incentives that undermined the independence necessary for objective financial oversight. The audit partners assigned to Enron were embedded within the company's culture to such an extent that they lost their ability to provide the skeptical, arms-length evaluation that professional auditing standards required.

Internal dissent at Enron was systematically discouraged through both formal and informal mechanisms. The rank-and-yank system created powerful incentives for conformity, as challenging prevailing assumptions or raising concerns about questionable practices could be interpreted as evidence of poor performance or insufficient commitment to the company's success. Employees who did raise concerns—such as Vice President Sherron Watkins, who wrote a detailed memo to Kenneth Lay warning of "an implosion waiting to happen"—faced retaliation, internal exile, and threats to their livelihoods.

This culture of silencing dissent reflected broader anthropological patterns observed in high-pressure organizational environments. When survival within an organization depends on maintaining the approval of superiors and peers, individuals develop sophisticated mechanisms for self-censorship and rationalization that allow them to suppress ethical concerns in favor of group cohesion and personal security. The psychological phenomenon of "motivated reasoning" explains how intelligent, well-intentioned individuals can convince themselves that questionable practices are acceptable when their livelihoods and identities are tied to organizational success.

The media relations strategy that Enron employed further reinforced its internal culture of deception by creating external validation for practices that might otherwise have been questioned internally. The company's charismatic leaders became fixtures on financial television networks and at industry conferences, projecting an image of innovation and success that made internal skepticism appear misguided or disloyal. This external validation created a feedback loop that reinforced the company's internal narrative while making it increasingly difficult for employees to voice concerns about practices that were being celebrated in the broader business community.

The technological infrastructure that Enron developed, particularly the EnronOnline trading platform launched in November 1999, represented both the pinnacle of Skilling's vision and the beginning of Enron's most dangerous period. The platform positioned Enron as a principal in every transaction, meaning that the company was taking the opposite side of every trade executed on the system. While this generated enormous trading volumes and apparent profits, it also concentrated unprecedented levels of risk within a single organization that lacked the capital base necessary to support such exposures.

The human cost of Enron's toxic culture extended far beyond the company's eventual bankruptcy. Employees who had devoted their careers to the organization found themselves not only unemployed but professionally stigmatized by association with one of the most notorious corporate scandals in American history. Many lost not only their jobs but also their retirement savings, which had been heavily concentrated in Enron stock through the company's 401(k) plan. The psychological trauma of discovering that their professional identities had been built on fraudulent foundations created lasting personal and social consequences that extended throughout the Houston business community and beyond.

The anthropological dimensions of Enron's failure reveal how organizational cultures can evolve in ways that systematically undermine the very values and practices necessary for long-term sustainability. The company's emphasis on short-term performance metrics and individual competition created an environment where collective welfare was subordinated to personal advancement, and where ethical considerations were viewed as obstacles to success rather than fundamental requirements for legitimate business operation.

Understanding Enron's internal failures requires recognizing that organizational cultures are not merely collections of individual choices but emergent properties of structural incentives, social dynamics, and leadership behaviors that interact in complex and often unpredictable ways. The transformation of Enron from a respected utility company into a vehicle for massive fraud was not the result of a few bad actors but the inevitable outcome of cultural and structural factors that made ethical behavior increasingly difficult and unethical behavior increasingly rational from the perspective of individual organizational members.

The lessons of Enron's internal failures extend far beyond the specific circumstances of that company to illuminate broader challenges facing modern corporations. The tension between short-term performance pressures and long-term sustainability, the difficulty of maintaining ethical standards in highly competitive environments, and the challenges of governing complex organizations in rapidly changing markets remain central concerns for corporate leaders, policymakers, and society as a whole.

The philosophical implications of Enron's internal culture point toward fundamental questions about the nature of moral responsibility in organizational contexts. When individual actors are embedded within systems that reward unethical behavior and punish ethical resistance, traditional notions of personal accountability become complicated by structural factors that shape and constrain individual choices. This recognition does not eliminate personal responsibility but suggests that preventing future Enrons requires attention not only to individual character but also to the organizational and social contexts that influence how that character is expressed in practice.

The legacy of Enron's internal failures continues to influence discussions of corporate culture, governance, and ethics more than two decades after the company's collapse. While regulatory reforms such as the Sarbanes-Oxley Act have addressed some of the technical vulnerabilities that Enron exploited, the deeper cultural and structural challenges that enabled the company's fraud to remain relevant concerns in contemporary corporate America. The ongoing occurrence of corporate scandals suggests that the lessons of Enron's internal failures have not been fully absorbed or translated into effective prevention mechanisms.

# Chapter Eight
## Regulatory and Oversight Results for Enron

The collapse of Enron in late 2001 revealed profound deficiencies in the regulatory and oversight framework of modern capitalism. Although much analysis has focused on the company's internal fraud, a comprehensive understanding demands scrutiny of the external environment that enabled and masked those deceptions. This chapter examines the impacts and loopholes of deregulation, the Securities and Exchange Commission's constraints, internal board failures, Arthur Andersen's conflicts and audit breakdowns, and the complicity of financial analysts and the media. An interdisciplinary lens—integrating legal philosophy, organizational theory, cognitive psychology, and systems analysis—reveals how rule-based systems and human limitations combined to create an environment in which Enron's fraudulent practices could flourish unchecked.

A mid-level SEC examiner once described spending weeks untangling dense Enron filings only to divert months to simpler cases—an anecdote that humanizes how complexity and resource constraints intersect in real offices.

Deregulation was foundational to Enron's rise. Beginning in the 1970s and accelerating through the 1980s and 1990s, U.S. policymakers embraced "neoliberal" principles that prioritized market efficiency and minimal government intervention. The Energy Policy Act of 1992 partially deregulated wholesale electricity markets, allowed energy brokers to operate without owning physical assets, and reduced price controls on natural gas. Similarly, the Telecommunications Act of 1996 eliminated barriers to entry in telecom and fostered aggressive competition. These reforms, while intended to spur innovation and lower consumer costs, also removed long-standing safeguards designed to prevent market abuses. Economic philosophies underpinning deregulation often assumed transparent markets and rational actors—assumptions betrayed by the complexity and asymmetry of modern financial products. This faith in market transparency ignored fundamental human limitations—our tendency to anchor on headline metrics and our discomfort with deep complexity—setting the stage for heuristics to substitute for oversight.

Enron capitalized on deregulation by expanding from pipeline operations into energy trading, broadband, and water services. The company's transition from a physical utility to a financialized trading empire depended on regulatory gaps it was uniquely positioned to exploit. Enron's executives routinely lobbied for further deregulation, framing constraints as impediments to innovation. The company's political influence and relationships with key legislators and regulators made it a powerful advocate for rule changes that favored complex trading structures over traditional oversight.

The U.S. Securities and Exchange Commission (SEC), charged with protecting investors and maintaining fair markets, struggled to keep pace with rapidly evolving financial innovations. From 1995 to 2000, the SEC's staff grew modestly while the number and complexity of corporate filings, derivatives, and trading volumes surged. Budget constraints and competing priorities meant that the SEC conducted fewer full-scale investigations per promulgated rule, creating "enforcement gaps" where sophisticated misstatements could persist. Philosophical perspectives on administrative law emphasize that regulatory effectiveness depends on both clear rules and sufficient enforcement capacity; the SEC's resource shortages rendered many complex transactions effectively unmonitored.

Legislative reforms compounded these enforcement challenges. The Private Securities Litigation Reform Act of 1995, designed to curb frivolous litigation, raised pleading standards for securities fraud and granted safe harbor for forward-looking statements. While reducing meritless lawsuits, the act also insulated companies from accountability when they made overly optimistic projections—projections Enron wielded to justify its aggressive mark-to-market accounting practices. By requiring plaintiffs to plead specific facts with particularity, the law made it more difficult to challenge management on abstract, complex financial arrangements.

Congressional oversight also failed. Despite high-profile hearings in 2001, Congress did not implement significant new regulatory measures until after Enron's collapse, reflecting both ideological divisions and insufficient technical understanding of complex energy derivatives. Philosophers of democratic governance argue that effective oversight requires both substantive expertise and political will—qualities in short supply during the late 1990s as Congress prioritized budgetary and geopolitical issues over financial regulation.

While external forces shaped the permissive terrain, Enron's internal culture planted the seeds for unchecked risk. The board and risk managers operated in an ecosystem where caution was socially sanctioned as defeatism.

At the corporate level, Enron's board of directors bore primary responsibility for governance and risk oversight. Comprised of prominent business leaders, academics, and former public officials, the board nevertheless lacked the specialized expertise required to assess Enron's novel trading strategies and complex financial vehicles. The board's audit, compensation, and risk committees met only quarterly, relying heavily on management representations without independent analysis. Organizational scholars note that deference to charismatic authority and groupthink can inhibit critical inquiry; Enron's board displayed both tendencies, overlooking red flags in favor of the company's performance narrative. The board's failures were exacerbated by inadequate risk management systems. Enron's Risk Assessment and Control (RAC) group, responsible for monitoring trading exposures, possessed sophisticated modeling capabilities but operated under cultural pressures that prioritized deal flow over caution. RAC analysts complained that rejecting profitable trades could endanger their performance reviews, illustrating how incentive structures can compromise control functions.

Arthur Andersen, Enron's auditor, exemplified the conflict-ridden consulting-audit model. Andersen derived nearly as much revenue from consulting services as from auditing, creating strong financial incentives to placate management. Andersen's Houston office developed a "client-first" ethos, tolerating document shredding and aggressive audit interpretations rather than jeopardize consulting fees. Andersen's destruction of Enron-related documents triggered obstruction of justice charges, leading to the firm's collapse. The Andersen case underscores how professional independence can be eroded by economic self-interest and group loyalty.

Financial analysts and the media also played enabling roles. Securities analysts, reliant on investment banking fees and consulting contracts, issued "strong buy" ratings on Enron stock despite growing complexity and opacity in the company's disclosures. Analysts faced direct pressure from deal teams to maintain positive coverage, illustrating institutional conflicts that compromise impartial research. The business media, eager for growth stories, replicated management's optimism without rigorous fact-checking, reinforcing investor confidence in Enron's narrative. These media dynamics reflect what communication scholars term "agenda-setting" and "access journalism"—the tendency for outlets to frame stories based on source availability and access rather than independent verification. Journalists bestowed untold coverage on Enron's innovations in energy trading and corporate culture, often based on management-provided materials and interviews. The resulting echo chamber inflated Enron's stock price, sustaining the company's market capitalization even as internal financial health deteriorated.

Regulatory capture further undermined enforcement. Enron maintained close relationships with key SEC officials through lobbying and employment pipelines. Senior SEC staff frequently joined private sector roles after leaving the agency, creating revolving-door dynamics that blurred boundaries between regulator and regulated. Philosophers of law warn that capture can transform agencies from public guardians into captive servants of industry, eroding public trust and reducing enforcement rigor.

International considerations provided additional avenues for evasion. Enron structured many transactions through offshore subsidiaries in jurisdictions with lax oversight, complicating cross-border regulatory cooperation. Transfer pricing and tax arbitrage strategies enabled Enron to shift profits to low-tax jurisdictions while evading consolidated reporting, exploiting inconsistencies in global accounting standards. These practices highlight the need for harmonized international regulation to address corporate mobility and complexity. Recent steps by the Basel Committee to unify bank-capital rules and by IOSCO to align derivative reporting show promising moves toward a more cohesive global guardrail.

From a systems theory perspective, Enron's regulatory and oversight failures represent interlocking feedback loops that escalated risks. Deregulation created new markets outside existing oversight; resource-strapped regulators failed to monitor emerging instruments; corporate boards deferred to executives hugging complex models; auditors prioritized fees over independence; analysts and media magnified management's narrative; and the revolving door reinforced industry influence over regulators. These loops generated escalating opacity until collapse became inevitable. A simple causal loop would show deregulation feeding complexity, which strains regulators, which defers to boards, which emboldens executives, closing the loop on opacity and collapse.

Anthropological and cognitive insights shed light on why these systemic failures persisted. Human cognitive biases—overconfidence in technical models, deference to authority, optimism in familiar sources—interacted with institutional incentives to suppress critical inquiry. Organizational cultures that valorized success and punished dissent made whistleblowing hazardous. Regulators and corporate directors, operating under resource and knowledge constraints, succumbed to satisficing behaviors, relying on heuristics rather than deep analysis.

The aftermath of Enron prompted significant reforms, most notably the Sarbanes-Oxley Act of 2002, which imposed stricter financial disclosure requirements, executive certifications of accuracy, enhanced penalties for fraud, and strengthened auditor independence rules. Public Company Accounting Oversight Board (PCAOB) oversight of auditors aimed to restore faith in external audits. Yet, while SOX addressed many technical deficiencies, it did less to reshape corporate culture and cognitive vulnerabilities that underpin corruption. Philosophers and ethicists argue that true reform requires values-based leadership, ethical training, and cultural transformation, not just tightened rules.

In conclusion, Enron's regulatory and oversight failures resulted from a complex interplay of deregulation biases, resource-constrained enforcement, board complacency, auditor conflicts, analyst and media complicity, regulatory capture, and global arbitrage. Addressing these multifaceted deficiencies demands comprehensive approaches that integrate structural reforms, cognitive interventions, cultural change, and international cooperation. Only by understanding both the technical and human dimensions of oversight can we build resilient systems capable of preventing the next Enron..

# Chapter Nine
## *The Collapse of Enron*

The downfall of Enron unfolded with astonishing rapidity in late 2001, transforming a Wall Street darling into a symbol of corporate malfeasance and systemic failure. By October 2001, investigative journalism and skeptical analysts had begun to expose the financial unraveling beneath the company's exuberant growth narrative. This chapter examines the gradual erosion of confidence through public exposure, the key milestones leading to Enron's bankruptcy, and the cascading human, economic, and political consequences that reshaped corporate governance, regulatory frameworks, and societal expectations of corporate conduct.

The transformation from celebrated energy innovator to cautionary tale began with seemingly routine financial disclosures that would trigger one of the most dramatic corporate collapses in American history. For months, astute observers had questioned the opacity of Enron's financial statements and the sustainability of its reported growth. Short-seller Jim Chanos had been betting against Enron stock since late 2000, convinced that the company's broadband division could not possibly outperform the struggling telecommunications sector. His analysis of Enron's cash flow statements revealed troubling patterns: despite reported profits, the company was burning through cash at an alarming rate while executives were selling their personal holdings at unprecedented levels.

Enron's financial unraveling began in earnest on October 16, 2001, when The Wall Street Journal published a front-page article questioning Enron's use of Special Purpose Entities (SPEs) and the accuracy of its earnings disclosures. The article, written by journalists John Emshwiller and Rebecca Smith, cited anonymous former employees who expressed grave concerns about off-balance-sheet obligations and the dependence of these entities on Enron's own stock price for their continued viability. One former executive was quoted as saying, "It's a house of cards built on Enron's stock price. If the stock falls, the whole thing comes tumbling down."

This initial exposé shattered the carefully constructed veneer of profitability that had sustained Enron's market valuation for years. Within hours of the article's publication, the stock price began its precipitous decline, falling from over $90 in mid-August 2001 to under $50 by mid-October. The role of investigative media in this phase highlights critical dynamics in modern financial markets: while Enron's sophisticated investor relations apparatus sought to reassure stakeholders through carefully orchestrated conference calls and press releases, journalists armed with anonymous tips and meticulous document analysis began to piece together inconsistencies that management could no longer dismiss or explain away.

The media investigation revealed the intricate web of relationships between Enron and the SPEs managed by Chief Financial Officer Andrew Fastow. These partnerships, with names like LJM, LJM2, and Chewco, were designed to appear independent while actually serving as repositories for Enron's debt and vehicles for manufacturing artificial profits. The journalists' work demonstrated how traditional accounting principles could be manipulated through complex financial engineering that disguised the true nature of corporate obligations and performance.

Simultaneously, financial analysts who had long endorsed Enron's stock began to revise their earnings estimates downward and issue more cautious recommendations. Merrill Lynch and Citigroup, both heavily involved in structuring Enron's SPEs and derivative transactions, faced profound conflicts of interest that initially delayed critical downgrades. These firms had earned substantial fees from helping create the very financial structures that were now being questioned, creating powerful incentives to maintain positive coverage even as evidence mounted that the company was in serious trouble.

Once the scale of hidden liabilities became undeniable, these firms cut their price targets sharply, exacerbating the decline in investor confidence. Behavioral finance theories illuminate this phenomenon as a form of "herd behavior" among analysts, driven by reputational concerns and institutional pressures that led to synchronized negative revisions. Rather than providing independent analysis, analysts clustered their recommendations, amplifying both the initial optimism that had inflated Enron's stock price and the subsequent pessimism that would accelerate its collapse.

As stockholders fled en masse, banks that had extended credit to Enron through various credit facilities invoked margin calls and drew down existing credit lines, precipitating severe liquidity pressures. Enron's once-vaunted access to commercial paper markets and bank financing abruptly vanished as counterparties sought to limit their exposure to a company whose financial condition was rapidly deteriorating. The rapidity of this reversal underscores a fundamental insight from systems theory: complex financial architectures that depend on continuous market confidence can become highly unstable when that confidence falters, creating feedback loops that transform temporary liquidity problems into permanent solvency crises.

The interconnectedness of modern financial markets meant that Enron's problems quickly spread beyond the company itself. Trading counterparties demanded additional collateral or simply refused to transact with Enron, limiting the company's ability to conduct its core energy trading business. Credit rating agencies, which had maintained investment-grade ratings on Enron debt through much of 2001, suddenly faced pressure to reassess their methodologies and explain how they had missed such massive financial problems.

By early November 2001, Enron had lost over 60 percent of its market value, severely eroding its ability to meet debt obligations and fund daily operations. The company's business model, which depended on maintaining investment-grade credit ratings to support its trading activities, was fundamentally incompatible with the market's growing skepticism about its financial condition. Credit rating agencies, previously hesitant to downgrade such a prominent company, issued downgrades to junk status, further limiting Enron's access to short-term financing and triggering cross-default clauses in numerous contracts.

The combination of market panic, credit withdrawal, and persistent revelations of accounting irregularities created a devastating feedback loop of decline that proved impossible to arrest. Corporate anthropology suggests that organizations under extreme crisis often experience rapid cultural disintegration, as collective denial gives way to fear, blame, and self-preservation instincts. Within Enron's Houston headquarters, employees reported increasingly frantic scenes: managers bypassed normal expense controls, emergency approvals for cash withdrawals soared, and the once-celebrated performance culture devolved into chaos as staff sought to salvage personal investments and career prospects.

The psychological impact on employees was severe. Many had concentrated their retirement savings in Enron stock, believing in the company's long-term prospects and encouraged by management's repeated assurances that the stock represented "an incredible bargain" at depressed prices. As the stock price continued to plummet, employees faced the double trauma of losing their jobs and watching their retirement savings evaporate simultaneously.

**Bankruptcy and Immediate Aftermath**

On November 8, 2001, Enron announced it would restate its earnings for the past four years, reducing reported net income by nearly $600 million and significantly increasing liabilities from previously unconsolidated SPEs. This admission of accounting errors represented a complete capitulation to the mounting evidence of financial manipulation that had been uncovered by journalists and analysts. The restatement triggered a 20 percent single-day stock decline and prompted trading in Enron bonds to be suspended as market makers struggled to assess the company's true financial condition.

Legislative oversight mechanisms quickly mobilized in response to the crisis. Congressional committees prepared to convene emergency hearings, key executives were subpoenaed to testify about their roles

THE "BABEL" THAT WAS ENRON

in the company's collapse, and federal prosecutors opened criminal investigations into potential securities fraud and conspiracy charges. The rapid governmental response reflected both the magnitude of Enron's failure and growing public outrage over what appeared to be systematic deception of investors, employees, and creditors.

One week after the earnings restatement, on November 15, 2001, Enron filed for bankruptcy protection under Chapter 11 of the U.S. Bankruptcy Code—the largest such filing in American history at that time—citing $63.4 billion in assets and $13.2 billion in debt. The swiftness of the filing conveyed not merely financial collapse but systemic contagion effects throughout the energy industry and broader financial markets. Thousands of trading counterparties faced contract terminations and potential losses, employees lost their jobs and retirement savings, and investors scrambled to assess residual equity value in what had become essentially worthless securities.

The Bankruptcy Code's provisions for corporate reorganization provided only temporary shelter from creditors and regulatory scrutiny. Enron's various business units were quickly evaluated for potential sale or spin-off, and it became clear that the parent entity would enter liquidation rather than successful reorganization. The company's most valuable assets—its natural gas pipelines and power plants—were sold to competitors and private equity firms, while its trading operations were effectively worthless without the credit ratings necessary to support counterparty relationships.

The immediate aftermath of the bankruptcy revealed the extensive human costs that are often obscured by balance sheet analysis and legal proceedings. Approximately 20,000 Enron employees lost their jobs, and many discovered that significant portions of their 401(k) retirement plans had been invested in Enron stock through company matching programs and employee stock purchase plans. This concentration of retirement assets in company stock, once viewed as evidence of employee confidence and alignment with shareholder interests, became a source of devastating financial loss when the stock became virtually worthless overnight.

Studies in occupational psychology document the severe consequences of sudden job loss combined with pension forfeiture, including increased rates of depression, anxiety, and long-term financial distress among affected individuals and families. Many Enron employees faced home foreclosures, were forced to delay children's educational plans, and experienced prolonged income insecurity that extended far beyond the immediate crisis. The psychological toll was compounded by the stigma associated with working for a company that had become synonymous with corporate fraud and deception.

These human impacts underscore fundamental principles of stakeholder theory in business ethics, which argues that corporate fiduciary duties extend beyond shareholder interests to encompass employee welfare, community impacts, and broader societal responsibilities. The concentration of employee retirement assets in company stock, while legally permissible and even encouraged through tax incentives, created conflicts of interest that prioritized theoretical employee-owner alignment over practical risk management and diversification principles.

**Economic and Market Consequences**

Economically, Enron's collapse contributed to a broader erosion of confidence in corporate governance and financial reporting that accelerated market volatility in late 2001. The Dow Jones Industrial Average fell by over 17 percent between mid-September and mid-November, partly in reaction to Enron's failure alongside the economic slowdown following the September 11 terrorist attacks. The combination of geopolitical uncertainty and corporate scandal created a particularly toxic environment for investor confidence and market stability.

The erosion of trust in financial intermediaries prompted institutional investors to fundamentally reevaluate their due diligence practices and asset allocation strategies. Pension fund managers, university endowments, and insurance companies that had relied on credit ratings and analyst recommendations found themselves questioning the reliability of traditional information sources and risk assessment methodologies. This institutional skepticism led to more conservative investment approaches and increased demand for transparency in corporate reporting.

The systemic implications extended far beyond Enron itself, as investors and regulators recognized that accounting scandals could trigger widespread market instability and undermine the fundamental mechanisms of capital allocation in modern economies. The revelation that major accounting firms, investment banks, and credit rating agencies had failed to detect or adequately warn about Enron's problems raised profound questions about the effectiveness of existing market governance structures.

Societal impacts reached into virtually every corner of American life through the interconnected nature of modern financial markets. Public pension funds managing retirement benefits for teachers, police officers, and other government employees saw significant portfolio losses from Enron holdings, constraining funding for public services and creating potential shortfalls in promised benefits. University endowments that had invested in Enron or energy sector funds experienced losses that affected research funding, scholarship programs, and educational initiatives.

Charitable foundations and nonprofit organizations faced similar challenges as Enron-related losses reduced their asset bases and constrained their ability to fund social programs and community development initiatives. The ripple effects demonstrated how corporate failures in one sector could compromise societal institutions and public goods far removed from the immediate business relationships.

Media analyses of the period suggest that the Enron debacle fundamentally reshaped the social contract between corporations and communities, elevating public expectations for corporate accountability and broader stakeholder engagement. The scandal eroded public trust in corporate leadership, the integrity of market institutions, and the effectiveness of regulatory oversight, fostering widespread cynicism about executive compensation, corporate philanthropy, and industry self-regulation narratives.

**Public and Political Reactions**

Politically, Enron's collapse spurred immediate and far-reaching legislative responses that would permanently alter the landscape of corporate governance and financial regulation. In late 2001 and early 2002, Congressional committees held extensive hearings on corporate governance failures, eliciting dramatic testimonies from former Enron executives, regulatory officials, and whistleblowers who had tried to warn about the company's problems.

The hearings featured memorable moments that crystallized public anger about corporate excess and regulatory failure. Kenneth Lay and Jeffrey Skilling's testimony, in which they largely denied responsibility for the company's collapse and claimed ignorance of the accounting manipulations that had hidden billions in debt, struck many observers as implausible and self-serving. Sherron Watkins, the Enron vice president who had warned Lay about potential accounting fraud in a detailed memo months before the collapse, became a celebrated whistleblower whose testimony highlighted the importance of internal dissent and ethical courage in corporate environments.

The pervasive narrative of executive greed and regulatory capture galvanized bipartisan support for comprehensive reform legislation. By mid-2002, the Sarbanes-Oxley Act (SOX) had emerged from Congressional deliberations as one of the most significant pieces of financial regulation since the New Deal era. SOX enacted stringent financial disclosure requirements, established the Public Company Accounting Oversight Board (PCAOB) to supervise auditing firms, and imposed personal certification requirements for CEO and CFO financial statements.

The legislation represented a fundamental philosophical shift toward rule-based accountability and enhanced deterrence mechanisms, moving away from the principle-based regulation and industry self-policing that had characterized the previous regulatory environment. Critics argued that while SOX addressed many technical vulnerabilities that Enron had exploited, it did not fully address the cultural and cognitive factors that had enabled the scandal, suggesting that compliance-focused reforms might be insufficient without broader changes in corporate culture and individual incentives.

Executive criminal prosecutions provided a parallel track for accountability and deterrence. Andrew Fastow, the chief financial officer who had orchestrated many of the SPE transactions, ultimately pled guilty to conspiracy charges and served six years in federal prison. Kenneth Lay and Jeffrey Skilling faced extensive criminal trials in 2005 and 2006, resulting in convictions for fraud, conspiracy, and securities violations. Lay's death from a heart attack in July 2006, prior to sentencing, led to the legal vacating of his convictions, while Skilling served more than twelve years in prison before his release in 2019.

These legal outcomes affirmed fundamental principles of personal liability for corporate wrongdoing and reinforced deterrence theory in criminal justice and corporate ethics. However, the complexity of financial crimes and the protracted appeals process led some observers to question whether the enormous costs of prosecution outweighed the societal benefits of deterrence, particularly given the difficulty of proving criminal intent in cases involving sophisticated accounting manipulations and complex corporate structures.

At the state level, Enron's legacy influenced pension fund regulations and educational curricula in business schools and professional programs. State regulators implemented new restrictions on the concentration of retirement plan assets in employer stock, mandated more extensive disclosure of investment risks, and enhanced fiduciary obligations for plan administrators. These reforms reflected growing recognition that protecting individual retirement security required active government intervention rather than reliance on market mechanisms and individual choice.

Universities revised accounting and finance programs to emphasize critical thinking, professional skepticism, and the social responsibilities of financial professionals. Case studies based on Enron's collapse became standard components of MBA curricula, ethics courses, and professional certification programs. These educational reforms reflected anthropological insights about cultural change, recognizing that sustainable transformation requires new narratives, training programs, and socialization processes to reshape cognitive schemas and behavioral norms among future business leaders.

**Civic and Institutional Responses**

Civic responses to Enron's collapse included significantly increased activity by watchdog organizations and nonprofit advocacy groups promoting corporate accountability and financial transparency. Organizations such as Public Citizen, the Project on Government Oversight, and the Center for Corporate Policy expanded their campaigns advocating for enhanced disclosure requirements, stronger whistleblower protections, and greater shareholder empowerment in corporate governance decisions.

These civic initiatives illustrated how civil society organizations can serve as important checks on both regulatory capture and corporate misconduct, providing alternative sources of information and analysis that complement formal oversight mechanisms. The advocacy community's response to Enron helped maintain public attention on corporate governance issues and provided ongoing pressure for implementation and enforcement of reform measures.

Professional organizations also underwent significant self-examination and reform in response to Enron's collapse. The American Institute of Certified Public Accountants revised its ethical guidelines and continuing education requirements, emphasizing the importance of auditor independence and professional skepticism. Law firms specializing in corporate governance developed new practice areas focused on compliance and risk management, reflecting growing demand for legal services related to regulatory compliance and internal controls.

The investment management industry implemented enhanced due diligence procedures and risk assessment methodologies, recognizing that traditional approaches to credit analysis and corporate evaluation had failed to identify Enron's problems despite numerous warning signs. These changes reflected broader shifts toward more skeptical and comprehensive approaches to investment analysis and portfolio risk management.

**Long-term Regulatory and Cultural Transformation**

As the immediate crisis subsided, long-term institutional responses emerged to address the systemic failures revealed by Enron's collapse. The Sarbanes-Oxley Act represented the most visible reform, but its implementation required extensive rulemaking, compliance system development, and cultural adaptation that continued for years after its enactment.

SOX established the Public Company Accounting Oversight Board (PCAOB) to provide independent oversight of auditing firms, mandate enhanced internal control reporting, and impose criminal penalties for executive misconduct in financial reporting. The law required CEOs and CFOs to personally certify the accuracy of financial statements and mandated that companies maintain effective internal controls over financial reporting. These measures partially addressed technical vulnerabilities in financial reporting and audit processes, demonstrating how rule-based reforms could close specific loopholes exposed by corporate fraud.

However, philosophical critiques noted that compliance alone could not ensure ethical conduct, as individuals might satisfy regulatory requirements while continuing to engage in questionable practices in other domains. Sustainable change required cultural transformation alongside regulatory tightening, recognizing that formal rules operate within broader social and organizational contexts that shape their interpretation and implementation.

Professional standards in accounting and auditing evolved significantly in response to the Arthur Andersen collapse and the conflicts of interest that had compromised Enron's financial oversight. The consulting-audit split became legally codified, restricting auditing firms from providing lucrative non-audit services to their audit clients. Professional accounting bodies revised codes of conduct to emphasize auditor independence, professional skepticism, and the duty to report irregularities to appropriate authorities.

Many firms implemented more rigorous quality control reviews, cross-office audit teams, and enhanced training programs to prevent the localized cultures of complacency that had enabled Andersen's failure at Enron. These organizational innovations reflected insights from systems theory about the importance of decentralizing decision-making and introducing redundant controls to increase institutional resilience against misconduct and capture.

Corporate governance practices underwent equally dramatic transformation in response to Enron's lessons. Boards of directors expanded their risk and audit committees, increased meeting frequency and duration, and actively recruited members with relevant technical expertise in accounting, finance, and risk management.

The era of purely ceremonial board service, characterized by limited time commitments and deference to management, gave way to more engaged and demanding oversight expectations.

Institutional investors and proxy advisory firms began demanding more transparent board disclosures and voting against directors perceived as ineffective or insufficiently independent. Stewardship codes in the United Kingdom and codes of best practice in other jurisdictions emphasized board accountability, comprehensive risk oversight, and meaningful engagement with diverse stakeholder groups beyond shareholders.

These governance changes aligned with stakeholder theory's emphasis on balancing shareholder interests with those of employees, creditors, communities, and society more broadly. The recognition that long-term value creation depends on maintaining broad-based trust and social license to operate represented a significant departure from the shareholder primacy model that had dominated corporate thinking during the 1990s.

**Cultural and Educational Impacts**

Culturally, the Enron scandal triggered extensive introspection within American business schools, corporate ethics programs, and professional development curricula across multiple industries. The case became a staple of MBA and law school classes, providing a comprehensive illustration of how technical expertise, incentive misalignments, cognitive biases, and ethical failures could interact to produce catastrophic outcomes.

Organizations incorporated values-based leadership training, ethical dilemma workshops, and "tone at the top" initiatives designed to embed integrity considerations into corporate decision-making processes. Behavioral ethics research informed these programs, demonstrating that ethical behavior could be strengthened through structured practices such as formal ethical deliberation, role-playing exercises, and commitment devices that activate individuals' moral identities while counteracting rationalization tendencies.

The development of comprehensive ethics and compliance programs became standard practice in large corporations, reflecting both regulatory requirements and genuine recognition that cultural factors played crucial roles in preventing misconduct. These programs typically included ethics training, reporting mechanisms for potential violations, investigation procedures, and disciplinary frameworks designed to create accountability for ethical behavior at all organizational levels.

**Industry-Specific Reforms**

The energy sector itself underwent significant structural changes in response to Enron's collapse and the broader recognition that deregulated markets required more sophisticated oversight mechanisms. Market regulators implemented tighter rules for energy derivatives trading, including mandatory registration of over-the-counter transactions and central clearing requirements designed to reduce counterparty risk and increase market transparency.

The Federal Energy Regulatory Commission (FERC) enhanced its market surveillance capabilities and substantially increased penalties for market manipulation, aiming to prevent the formation of artificial trading schemes that had enabled some of Enron's deceptive practices. These regulatory improvements reflected growing understanding that competitive markets required active oversight to prevent abuse and maintain fair pricing mechanisms.

Organizational models in the energy industry shifted toward greater vertical integration and longer-term contracting relationships, reducing reliance on speculative trading activities that had characterized Enron's business model. Companies emphasized operational excellence and asset ownership over financial engineering, reflecting both regulatory pressure and market demands for more transparent and sustainable business models.

**Global Regulatory Harmonization**

Internationally, Enron's failure prompted significant efforts toward global regulatory harmonization and cooperation in financial oversight. The International Organization of Securities Commissions (IOSCO) and the International Accounting Standards Board (IASB) accelerated efforts to converge U.S. Generally Accepted Accounting Principles (GAAP) with International Financial Reporting Standards (IFRS), aiming to reduce regulatory arbitrage opportunities and improve consistency in financial reporting across jurisdictions.

The G20 and Financial Stability Board developed comprehensive principles for sound corporate governance, audit oversight, and financial market regulation, recognizing that multinational corporations and integrated financial markets required coordinated regulatory responses to prevent systemic risks from emerging in regulatory gaps or jurisdictional conflicts.

These global initiatives reflected systems thinking about financial regulation, acknowledging that in an interconnected world economy, weaknesses in one jurisdiction's regulatory framework could propagate globally through cross-border capital flows, multinational corporate structures, and integrated financial markets.

**Ongoing Challenges and Limitations**

Despite extensive reforms, significant challenges persisted in addressing the root causes of corporate misconduct and systemic risk. The phenomenon of "ethical forgetting" in organizational settings meant that Enron's lessons gradually faded from collective memory as new personnel entered organizations and immediate crisis pressures subsided. This natural decay in institutional memory created ongoing risks that similar problems could emerge in new forms or different contexts.

Continued financial innovation, including complex structured products, algorithmic trading systems, and emerging digital assets, recreated many of the opacity and risk concentration issues that had characterized Enron's collapse. Cognitive biases such as overconfidence, confirmation bias, and groupthink remained inherent features of human decision-making, requiring ongoing vigilance and institutional safeguards rather than one-time reforms.

Subsequent corporate scandals and financial crises demonstrated that the fundamental tensions between short-term performance pressures and long-term sustainability, between individual incentives and collective welfare, and between innovation and risk management continued to challenge corporate governance systems and regulatory frameworks.

The collapse of Enron catalyzed the most comprehensive set of corporate governance and financial regulatory reforms since the Great Depression, touching every aspect of how public companies operate, report their financial condition, and interact with stakeholders. The scandal's legacy underscores the critical importance of interdisciplinary approaches to understanding and preventing corporate misconduct, integrating insights from law, economics, psychology, anthropology, and systems theory to address the multiple dimensions of organizational failure.

The reforms that emerged from Enron's collapse—enhanced disclosure requirements, stronger audit oversight, more engaged corporate governance, and cultural emphasis on ethical behavior—represented significant progress in addressing the technical and structural vulnerabilities that had enabled the company's fraud. However, the persistence of corporate scandals and systemic risks in subsequent years demonstrates that preventing future Enrons requires ongoing attention to the complex interactions between regulatory frameworks, organizational cultures, individual incentives, and cognitive limitations that shape behavior in corporate environments.

Understanding Enron's rapid unraveling and its aftermath provides essential insights for navigating the continuing challenges of corporate governance, financial regulation, and ethical leadership in an increasingly complex and interconnected global economy. The lessons learned from this catastrophic failure must continue to inform efforts to build more resilient, accountable, and trustworthy institutions capable of serving broader societal interests while maintaining the innovation and efficiency that characterize healthy market economies.

# Chapter Ten
## Sarbanes Oxley Act and Regulatory Reform

The summer of 2002 was heavy with disillusionment. In Washington, the marble halls of Congress echoed with a rare urgency. The nation had just watched Enron implode in a storm of shredded paper and vanished pensions, only to see WorldCom follow with an accounting fraud so vast it made Enron look almost modest. The nightly news carried images of executives raising their right hands and then refusing to answer questions, auditors fumbling to explain why truckloads of documents had been destroyed, and employees testifying about the evaporation of their life savings. The spectacle was not just financial; it was moral. Americans who had been told that markets were self-correcting now wondered whether the entire system was a stage set, a Potemkin village of numbers.

The WorldCom revelation had come in June 2002, just as the nation was beginning to absorb the lessons of Enron's collapse. Bernie Ebbers, WorldCom's charismatic CEO, had built a telecommunications empire through aggressive acquisitions and accounting manipulations that would eventually total $11 billion in fraudulent entries. The company had systematically capitalized operating expenses, inflating earnings and misleading investors about the true state of its finances. When the fraud was exposed, WorldCom's bankruptcy filing dwarfed even Enron's, making it the largest corporate failure in American history to that point.

The convergence of these scandals created a perfect storm of public outrage and political necessity. Corporate executives had become objects of public scorn, their perp walks and Congressional testimony broadcast into American living rooms with the regularity of a prime-time television series. The images were searing: Kenneth Lay taking the Fifth Amendment, Arthur Andersen partners explaining the routine destruction of documents, WorldCom's Scott Sullivan detailing the mechanical process of moving billions from one accounting category to another.

Media coverage intensified the sense of betrayal felt by ordinary Americans. Local newspapers ran stories about municipal pension funds devastated by Enron holdings, teachers' retirement systems gutted by WorldCom investments, and families whose 401(k) plans had evaporated along with their employers' stock prices. The personal became political as constituents demanded answers from representatives who had championed deregulation and celebrated the new economy's financial innovations.

The hearings were theater, but theater with consequences. Senators who had once toasted deregulation now spoke of betrayal. Representative Michael Oxley, a Republican from Ohio, and Senator Paul Sarbanes, a Democrat from Maryland, found themselves unlikely partners in a moment of bipartisan necessity. Their names would be forever linked to the law that emerged: the Sarbanes-Oxley Act of 2002. It was rushed through with unusual speed, signed by President George W. Bush in July, and hailed as the most sweeping corporate reform since the New Deal.

The legislative process itself reflected the extraordinary circumstances that had created the political opportunity for reform. Oxley, a former FBI agent turned legislator, had spent years advocating for market-friendly policies and opposing regulatory expansion. His committee had been instrumental in advancing the Private Securities Litigation Reform Act of 1995, which had weakened shareholder lawsuits and reduced corporate liability for forward-looking statements. Yet by 2002, even Oxley recognized that the pendulum had swung too far toward deregulation and that investor confidence required visible government action.

Sarbanes brought different credentials to the partnership. A former federal prosecutor with deep expertise in securities law, he had long advocated for stronger investor protections and more robust corporate governance standards. His Senate Banking Committee had conducted some of the most penetrating investigations into the Enron collapse, eliciting testimony that revealed the systematic nature of the company's deceptions and the failures of its oversight mechanisms.

The bipartisan cooperation that produced Sarbanes-Oxley was remarkable for its speed and comprehensiveness. In an era of increasing political polarization, corporate scandal had created a rare zone of agreement. Republicans recognized that market capitalism required public trust to function effectively, while Democrats seized the opportunity to implement reforms they had long advocated. The legislation passed the House by a vote of 423-3 and the Senate 99-0, reflecting the extraordinary consensus that had emerged around the need for comprehensive reform.

The law's provisions were designed to strike at the very weaknesses exposed by Enron and Andersen. The creation of the Public Company Accounting Oversight Board was a quiet revolution: for the first time, auditors themselves would be subject to inspection and discipline. CEOs and CFOs were required to personally certify financial statements, a direct rebuke to the spectacle of executives pleading ignorance. Section 404 mandated internal controls and auditor attestation, recognizing that fraud often hides in the shadows of weak systems. Whistleblower protections were a nod to Sherron Watkins, the Enron vice president who had raised alarms internally but found little support. Criminal penalties for document destruction were a direct answer to Andersen's shredding frenzy.

The PCAOB represented perhaps the most significant institutional innovation in the legislation. For decades, the accounting profession had regulated itself through the American Institute of Certified Public Accountants and various peer review mechanisms that had proven inadequate to prevent the conflicts of interest and quality failures revealed by the Enron scandal. The new board would have authority to set auditing standards, conduct inspections of auditing firms, and impose disciplinary sanctions for substandard performance.

The board's structure reflected careful attention to the independence problems that had compromised self-regulation. Board members were prohibited from practicing public accounting during their tenure, and the majority were required to be non-accountants to ensure external perspective. Funding would come from assessments on public companies rather than from the accounting firms being regulated, eliminating the financial dependence that had undermined previous oversight efforts.

Section 302 of the act required CEO and CFO certification of financial statements, creating personal accountability that had been absent in previous regulatory frameworks. The certification requirements went beyond simply affirming the accuracy of financial statements to include assertions about the effectiveness of internal controls and the absence of material weaknesses in financial reporting systems. These requirements were designed to eliminate the "ostrich defense" that had allowed executives to claim ignorance of problems in their organizations.

The cultural shift was immediate. In boardrooms across America, the mood changed. A Fortune 500 CEO, preparing to sign his first certification under the new law, reportedly spent an entire weekend combing through financial statements line by line. "I'm not going to jail for this," he told his staff. The remark, half joking, half terrified, captured the new reality: accountability was no longer abstract. Boards, too, began to change. Audit committees, once perfunctory, became central. Directors who had once nodded politely through management presentations now demanded detailed explanations. The ritual oversight that had characterized Enron's board was replaced, at least in part, by genuine scrutiny.

The transformation of corporate boards was one of the most visible and immediate effects of the new legislation. Directors who had viewed their roles as largely ceremonial suddenly found themselves facing substantial legal and reputational risks if they failed to exercise proper oversight. Board meetings became longer and more substantive, with directors spending significantly more time reviewing financial statements, internal control reports, and risk assessments.

Compensation for board service increased substantially as the responsibilities and risks associated with directorship expanded. Companies began actively recruiting directors with specific expertise in accounting, finance, and risk management, moving away from the celebrity directors and social connections that had characterized many boards during the 1990s. The era of the purely ornamental board was ending, replaced by more professional and engaged oversight bodies.

The PCAOB's first inspections revealed just how necessary oversight was. Inspectors walked into Big Four offices in 2003 and were met with hostility. "We've never had anyone check our work," one partner muttered. The inspectors found sloppy documentation, overreliance on management's word, and a culture that had confused client service with complicity. It was a moment of reckoning for a profession that had forgotten its public duty.

The inspection process revealed systemic weaknesses that went far beyond the specific failures at Arthur Andersen. Auditing firms had developed cultures that prioritized client satisfaction over professional skepticism, viewing their primary obligation as helping companies present their financial results in the most favorable light rather than ensuring accurate and complete disclosure to investors. Work papers were often incomplete or missing, audit procedures were frequently abbreviated or skipped entirely, and quality control systems were inadequate to detect and correct deficiencies.

The PCAOB's early inspection reports, while heavily redacted to protect proprietary information, painted a picture of a profession in need of fundamental reform. Inspectors found that auditors routinely accepted management explanations without sufficient corroborating evidence, failed to adequately test internal controls, and overlooked obvious red flags that should have triggered additional scrutiny. The reports documented a pattern of superficial compliance with professional standards rather than the rigorous investigation that effective auditing required.

Whistleblowers, too, began to test the law. In 2004, a mid-level accountant at a technology firm invoked SOX after being demoted for raising concerns about revenue recognition. The case went to court, and the company was forced to reinstate him. The precedent was small but significant: employees now had a legal shield, however imperfect. Hannah Arendt's reflections on responsibility resonate here. Arendt warned that bureaucracies often diffuse accountability, making it easy for individuals to say they were "just following orders." SOX, by protecting dissenters, sought to pierce that diffusion. It gave individuals a reason to resist conformity, to speak when silence was easier.

The whistleblower provisions of Sarbanes-Oxley represented a significant departure from previous approaches to corporate misconduct, which had relied primarily on external detection through audits, regulatory examinations, and market mechanisms. The legislation recognized that employees were often the first to become aware of fraudulent or questionable practices and that protecting their ability to report such concerns was essential to preventing future scandals.

The protection extended beyond simple job security to include broader forms of retaliation such as blacklisting, harassment, and discrimination. The Department of Labor was given authority to investigate complaints and order remedies, including reinstatement, back pay, and compensation for litigation costs. These provisions created a framework for encouraging internal reporting while protecting individuals who took the significant personal and professional risks associated with challenging their employers.

Yet the law was not without controversy. Section 404 became infamous for its costs. Companies spent millions documenting and testing controls. For large firms, the expense was manageable; for smaller companies, it was crushing. A mid-cap CFO complained in 2005 that he was spending more time proving his honesty than running his business. Compliance teams ballooned, auditors demanded exhaustive documentation, and executives grumbled that the law was stifling entrepreneurial energy. Lon Fuller's principle of congruence is instructive here: laws must be workable in practice, not just noble in aspiration. A law that is too burdensome risks undermining its own legitimacy. Herbert Simon's concept of bounded rationality also applies. Executives and auditors, already stretched, now had to process mountains of compliance data, sometimes at the expense of judgment. The danger was that the form of compliance could eclipse its substance.

The implementation of Section 404 proved to be one of the most contentious aspects of the entire Sarbanes-Oxley framework. Companies discovered that documenting and testing internal controls required massive investments in personnel, systems, and external consulting services. The initial cost estimates, which had suggested that compliance would require relatively modest expenditures, proved to be wildly optimistic as companies grappled with the practical requirements of comprehensive control documentation and testing.

Large companies typically spent millions of dollars in the first year of compliance, hiring armies of consultants to map business processes, identify control points, and design testing procedures. The Big Four accounting firms saw their advisory revenues surge as companies desperate to achieve compliance turned to the same firms that had previously provided audit services. This created new potential conflicts of interest as consulting engagements sometimes influenced the independence of audit relationships.

Smaller public companies faced even greater challenges, as they lacked the resources and infrastructure to absorb the compliance costs without significant impact on their operations and profitability. Many smaller firms found that Section 404 compliance consumed substantial management time and attention, diverting resources from business development and strategic planning. Some companies chose to go private rather than bear the ongoing costs of public company compliance, contributing to a decline in the number of publicly traded companies in the United States.

And yet Sarbanes-Oxley did not remain confined to the shadow of Enron. In the years that followed, its provisions were tested in courtrooms and boardrooms far removed from Houston. The law acquired a second life, invoked in scandals that bore little resemblance to Enron but revealed the same temptations of power and the same fragility of trust.

The adaptability of the Sarbanes-Oxley framework to address diverse forms of corporate misconduct demonstrated the legislation's fundamental soundness and broad applicability. Rather than being narrowly tailored to address only the specific problems revealed by Enron and WorldCom, the law had created institutional mechanisms and accountability frameworks that could be applied to a wide range of corporate governance challenges.

The first great test came with HealthSouth. Richard Scrushy, the company's flamboyant CEO, was indicted for a massive accounting fraud, and prosecutors seized on the brand-new certification requirement. Scrushy had signed financial statements that prosecutors claimed he knew were false. Though he was acquitted on those counts, the trial dramatized the new reality: a chief executive's signature was no longer ceremonial. It was a legal oath, binding him personally to the truth of the numbers. Even in acquittal, the shadow of accountability had lengthened.

The HealthSouth case revealed both the potential and the limitations of the certification requirements. While Scrushy's acquittal on the federal securities fraud charges demonstrated the continued difficulty of proving executive knowledge and intent in complex financial fraud cases, the extensive litigation and reputational damage associated with the charges illustrated the new risks that executives faced under the enhanced accountability framework.

The case also highlighted the importance of corporate culture in determining the effectiveness of legal reforms. HealthSouth's problems extended far beyond technical accounting issues to encompass a broader pattern of aggressive financial reporting, inadequate internal controls, and a corporate culture that prioritized meeting earnings expectations over accurate financial reporting. The Sarbanes-Oxley reforms could address some of these issues through enhanced disclosure and certification requirements, but they could not directly mandate changes in corporate culture and values.

Whistleblowers, too, began to push the law's boundaries. In Lawson v. FMR (2014), the Supreme Court held that SOX's protections extended not only to employees of public companies but also to those working for their contractors and subcontractors. Suddenly, the shield covered a far wider circle of dissenters. The decision broadened the cultural impact of SOX: it gave voice to those who might otherwise have been silenced by hierarchy or fear. The law had become a statutory megaphone for conscience.

The Lawson decision represented a significant expansion of the whistleblower protection framework, recognizing that modern corporate structures often involve complex relationships between parent companies, subsidiaries, contractors, and other business partners. The Court's interpretation acknowledged that fraud and misconduct often involve multiple entities and that protecting whistleblowers only within the narrow confines of direct employment relationships would leave significant gaps in the protective framework.

This expansion of coverage reflected broader changes in how corporations organize their operations and manage their relationships with external service providers. The increasing use of outsourcing, subcontracting, and other forms of business partnering meant that important corporate functions were often performed by individuals who were not technically employees of the public companies whose securities could be affected by misconduct.

The PCAOB itself became a subject of constitutional drama. In Free Enterprise Fund v. PCAOB (2010), challengers argued that the Board was too insulated from presidential control. The Court upheld its existence but struck down part of its structure. The case revealed the tension at the heart of SOX: how much independence should watchdogs have from political control? Oversight, it seemed, was always contested—whether by accountants resisting inspectors or by lawyers arguing separation of powers.

The constitutional challenge to the PCAOB reflected broader debates about the proper structure of administrative agencies and the extent to which regulatory independence could be reconciled with democratic accountability. The challengers argued that the Board's dual-layer protection from removal—Board members could only be removed by the SEC, which was itself an independent agency—violated the constitutional principle of executive control over administrative agencies.

The Supreme Court's decision in Free Enterprise Fund struck down the dual-layer protection while preserving the PCAOB's essential functions and authority. The ruling required that Board members be subject to removal by the SEC without cause, but it maintained the Board's independence from the accounting firms it regulated and preserved its authority to conduct inspections, set standards, and impose disciplinary sanctions.

Then came the case that bordered on the absurd. In Yates v. United States (2015), a Florida fisherman who had thrown undersized grouper overboard was prosecuted under SOX's anti-shredding provision. The statute, written to prevent the destruction of financial records, was suddenly being used to punish the disposal of fish. The Supreme Court balked, ruling that "tangible objects" in SOX meant records and documents, not marine life. The episode became a parable of overreach: a law born of corporate scandal stretched so far it risked ridicule.

The Yates case illustrated the dangers of overly broad statutory language and prosecutorial overreach in applying corporate crime statutes to situations far removed from their intended purposes. The government's attempt to apply the document destruction provisions of Sarbanes-Oxley to fish disposal demonstrated how general language designed to address corporate misconduct could be stretched to cover conduct that bore no meaningful relationship to the problems the legislation was intended to solve.

The Supreme Court's narrow interpretation of the "tangible objects" language reflected a broader judicial concern about the expansion of federal criminal law and the tendency of prosecutors to apply corporate crime statutes in contexts that exceeded their intended scope. The decision reinforced the principle that criminal statutes should be interpreted narrowly and that prosecutors should exercise restraint in charging decisions involving ambiguous statutory language.

And yet, the law endured. In Murray v. UBS Securities (2024), the Court reaffirmed SOX's whistleblower protections, underscoring that two decades later, the statute still framed the balance between loyalty to employers and loyalty to truth. The case involved a research analyst who alleged retaliation for refusing to skew reports. The Court sided with the whistleblower, reminding corporate America that the spirit of SOX was alive: the protection of integrity against the pressures of profit.

The Murray decision demonstrated the continued vitality of the Sarbanes-Oxley framework more than twenty years after its enactment. The case involved allegations that a securities analyst had been retaliated against for refusing to alter research reports to present a more favorable view of investment opportunities. The analyst claimed that supervisors had pressured him to modify his conclusions to align with the firm's business interests rather than his independent professional judgment.

The Supreme Court's decision in favor of the whistleblower reinforced the principle that the integrity of financial markets depends on the independence and honesty of market participants, including research analysts whose reports influence investor decisions. The ruling demonstrated that Sarbanes-Oxley's whistleblower protections remain relevant in addressing new forms of market misconduct and conflicts of interest that continue to emerge in evolving financial markets.

Taken together, these cases trace the arc of a law that outlived its scandal. HealthSouth showed the difficulty of convicting executives but also the new seriousness of certification. Lawson and Murray expanded the moral space for dissent. Free Enterprise Fund tested the boundaries of regulatory independence. Yates revealed the dangers of overextension. Each episode was a mirror, reflecting both the promise and the limits of legislating ethics. Law cannot manufacture virtue, but without it, the space for virtue shrinks. Sarbanes-Oxley's afterlife thus became a meditation on the paradox of reform: imperfect, sometimes overreaching, but indispensable in the ongoing struggle to align law, culture, and conscience.

The jurisprudential evolution of Sarbanes-Oxley reflected broader themes in the relationship between law and corporate behavior. Each case that interpreted and applied the statute contributed to a growing body of precedent that shaped how companies, executives, and employees understood their obligations and protections under the new regulatory framework. The law became a living document, continually refined and adapted through judicial interpretation and practical application.

This evolutionary process demonstrated both the strengths and limitations of legislative responses to corporate scandals. While Sarbanes-Oxley provided important tools for addressing misconduct and protecting whistleblowers, its effectiveness ultimately depended on how these tools were used by prosecutors, courts, regulators, and private parties. The law created possibilities for accountability and deterrence, but it could not guarantee that these possibilities would be realized in every case.

Nor was its influence confined to America. Across the Atlantic, Europe was experiencing its own corporate traumas—Parmalat in Italy, Ahold in the Netherlands, Vivendi in France. These scandals made clear that the vulnerabilities exposed by Enron were not uniquely American. The European Commission responded in 2003 with its Action Plan on Modernizing Company Law and Enhancing Corporate Governance, explicitly acknowledging that it shared "the same broad objectives and principles" as SOX, even if Europe's legal traditions differed.

The Parmalat scandal in Italy involved accounting fraud and financial manipulation on a scale that rivaled Enron and WorldCom, with missing assets eventually totaling over €14 billion. The company had used a complex web of offshore subsidiaries and financial instruments to hide losses and inflate revenues, creating fictitious assets and transactions that misled investors and creditors about the company's true financial condition. The scandal exposed weaknesses in Italian corporate governance, auditing standards, and regulatory oversight that paralleled many of the problems revealed by the American corporate scandals.

Similarly, the Royal Ahold scandal in the Netherlands involved inflated earnings and improper accounting that ultimately required restatements totaling billions of euros. The company had used aggressive acquisition accounting and vendor allowance manipulation to meet earnings targets and maintain its growth trajectory, demonstrating that the pressure to meet market expectations could lead to similar misconduct regardless of national context or corporate culture.

The Vivendi scandal in France revealed how media and telecommunications conglomerates could use complex corporate structures and accounting techniques to obscure their true financial condition and operational performance. The company's aggressive expansion strategy and creative financial reporting eventually led to massive write-downs and management changes that paralleled the corporate upheavals experienced by American companies during the same period.

Where the U.S. had chosen a rules-based, enforcement-oriented approach, Europe leaned toward its familiar "comply or explain" model: companies were expected to follow governance codes or justify their deviations. Yet the influence of SOX was unmistakable. The EU began harmonizing disclosure rules, strengthening audit oversight, and clarifying director liability. Audit committees became more independent, echoing SOX's insistence on financial expertise. The Commission's reforms sought to balance efficiency with accountability, recognizing that Europe's bank-centered, block-holding corporate structures required a different calibration than America's dispersed ownership model.

The European approach to corporate governance reform reflected different institutional traditions and ownership structures that had evolved over decades of distinct legal and economic development. Continental European companies typically featured concentrated ownership through banks, families, or government entities, creating different agency problems and governance challenges than the dispersed ownership model that characterized American public companies.

The "comply or explain" framework allowed companies to deviate from recommended governance practices as long as they provided transparent explanations for their choices, creating flexibility while maintaining accountability. This approach reflected European preferences for principles-based regulation and stakeholder-oriented corporate governance that balanced shareholder interests with those of employees, creditors, and communities.

In the United Kingdom, already proud of its Combined Code, tightened its requirements for independent directors and audit committees, insisting that boards demonstrate not just formal compliance but genuine oversight. Germany revised its Corporate Governance Code, emphasizing transparency, shareholder rights, and the duty of supervisory boards to challenge management. Italy, still reeling from the Parmalat scandal, introduced stricter auditing and disclosure rules, determined to prevent another national embarrassment. France strengthened its rules on financial disclosure and board accountability, while the Netherlands, scarred by Ahold, moved to reinforce auditor independence.

The German response was particularly significant given the country's distinctive two-tier board structure, which separated supervisory and management functions in ways that differed substantially from Anglo-American governance models. The German Corporate Governance Code had to address how supervisory boards could exercise more effective oversight while respecting the traditional division of responsibilities between supervisory and executive functions.

The Italian reforms went beyond technical compliance requirements to address broader issues of corporate culture and market integrity. The Parmalat scandal had revealed not only accounting fraud but also failures of regulatory oversight, market intermediation, and investor protection that required comprehensive institutional reforms rather than narrow technical fixes.

French reforms reflected the country's unique combination of state influence, concentrated ownership, and global market participation. The changes had to balance traditional French approaches to corporate governance with international expectations for transparency and accountability that had been heightened by the global wave of corporate scandals.

Each country adapted the lessons of Enron and SOX to its own traditions, but the pattern was unmistakable: a continental shift toward stronger boards, more independent auditors, and greater transparency. Europe did not simply copy the American model; it translated it into its own idiom of "comply or explain," blending hard law with soft norms. Yet the influence of Sarbanes-Oxley was everywhere, a transatlantic echo that reminded regulators and investors alike that trust, once broken, had to be rebuilt with visible reforms.

The adaptation process demonstrated how legal and regulatory innovations could spread across different institutional contexts while being modified to fit local conditions and preferences. The core insights of Sarbanes-Oxley—the importance of independent oversight, personal accountability, and whistleblower protection—proved to be broadly applicable across different legal systems and corporate structures.

By the late 2000s, the European Union had adopted directives on audit oversight, cross-border mergers, and shareholder rights that bore the imprint of SOX's hard lessons. The International Accounting Standards Board and IOSCO pushed for convergence between U.S. GAAP and IFRS, narrowing the space for arbitrage. The G20 and Financial Stability Board, in the wake of the 2008 crisis, emphasized principles for sound governance that echoed both SOX and Europe's codes.

The convergence efforts reflected growing recognition that global capital markets required consistent standards and compatible regulatory frameworks to function effectively. Companies operating across multiple jurisdictions needed clarity about their obligations, while investors required confidence that similar standards of disclosure and accountability applied regardless of where securities were issued or traded.

The 2008 financial crisis provided additional impetus for international coordination, as policymakers recognized that corporate governance failures could contribute to systemic risks that transcended national boundaries. The crisis demonstrated that problems in one country's financial system could rapidly spread to others through interconnected markets and institutions, making international cooperation essential for maintaining global financial stability.

In this way, Sarbanes-Oxley became not just an American statute but a global reference point. It was cited in Brussels, debated in Frankfurt, adapted in Tokyo, and studied in London. Its spirit—the insistence that trust requires law, and that oversight must be credible—seeped into the DNA of global corporate governance.

The global influence of Sarbanes-Oxley extended beyond formal regulatory adoption to encompass broader changes in corporate culture, professional standards, and market expectations. Companies operating in international markets found that investors and stakeholders increasingly expected governance practices that met SOX-like standards regardless of formal legal requirements. This created competitive pressures for transparency and accountability that supplemented formal regulatory mandates.

Professional service firms, particularly accounting and consulting firms, developed global practices and methodologies that reflected SOX principles and requirements. These firms became important transmission mechanisms for spreading SOX-influenced governance practices throughout the global business community, as they advised clients on best practices and compliance requirements across multiple jurisdictions.

The legislation's impact on business school curricula, professional training programs, and corporate culture initiatives created long-term effects that extended far beyond immediate compliance requirements. A generation of business leaders was trained to understand corporate governance through frameworks that had been fundamentally shaped by the Sarbanes-Oxley experience, ensuring that the law's influence would persist even as specific regulatory requirements evolved.

Twenty years after its enactment, Sarbanes-Oxley remains one of the most significant and enduring pieces of corporate governance legislation in modern history. Its influence extends far beyond the specific scandals that prompted its creation to encompass fundamental changes in how corporations are governed, how financial markets operate, and how societies think about the relationship between business and accountability. The law's legacy demonstrates both the potential and the limitations of legislative responses to corporate misconduct, while its global influence illustrates how domestic reforms can reshape international standards and practices in an interconnected world economy.

# Chapter Eleven
## The Anthropological and Psychological Dimensions of Corporate Failure

**Fragmented Vigilance**

Humans evolved as small-group foragers reliant on distributed vigilance—or "sentinel awareness"—to detect immediate threats such as predators or rival bands. In these contexts, individuals specialized in scanning for danger took on watch-duty shifts, alerting the group to risks beyond an individual's perceptual range. This division of labor leveraged mutual dependence: each member trusted that others would raise alarms when needed.

The effectiveness of this ancestral vigilance system depended on several key factors: clear communication channels between sentinels, shared understanding of what constituted a threat, and immediate consequences for failing to maintain watch. When a sentinel spotted a predator or hostile group, the alarm would spread rapidly through the entire band, triggering coordinated defensive responses that maximized survival chances for all members.

In modern corporations, however, the hazards to organizational survival are abstract—hidden liabilities, opaque derivatives, and regulatory shifts—yet the vigilance model remains decentralized. At Enron, departments acted as isolated sentinels: trading desks monitored market risks; legal teams advised on contract terms; auditors examined financial statements; and the board oversaw macro-risks. Critically, no integrated mechanism existed to synthesize warnings from these "lookouts."

The corporate structure at Enron created what systems theorists call "functional silos"—specialized units that excelled within their domains but lacked comprehensive oversight mechanisms. Unlike ancestral sentinel systems where all watchers shared the same survival imperative and operated within visual or auditory range of each other, Enron's departmental structure created physical and informational barriers that prevented holistic risk assessment.

When frontline traders reported underperforming contracts to their managers, the information rarely reached risk committees that focused on credit exposure rather than accounting irregularities. Legal memos highlighted questionable SPE structures, but compliance officers deferred to internal tax advisors versed in regulatory arbitrage rather than ethics. Auditors flagged atypical transactions, yet Andersen's client-first culture and revenue incentives prevented rigorous follow-up. The board's risk committee received quarterly summaries rather than real-time alerts, while the audit committee, meeting only periodically, depended on management's sanitized presentations.

This fragmentation created blind spots analogous to a hunting party trusting multiple sentinels in different directions but lacking a communal watchtower. The metaphor becomes even more apt when considering that ancestral sentinel systems included backup mechanisms—multiple watchers covering overlapping territories, regular rotation to prevent fatigue, and social sanctions for those who failed in their vigilance duties. Enron lacked all of these protective redundancies.

Without a central system to pool disparate alerts, no collective situational awareness emerged until fraud had already metastasized. The tragedy was not that warning signals were absent, but that they were scattered across organizational boundaries that prevented synthesis and coordinated response.

### Cognitive Shortcuts and Heuristic Failures

Cognitive limitations amplify this structural fragmentation. Neuroscientific research shows that the human brain excels at pattern recognition within familiar contexts—faces, social hierarchies, immediate physical dangers—but struggles with complex abstractions such as nested financial derivatives or layered off-balance-sheet entities.

The human visual system, for instance, can instantly detect a human face in a crowd or identify the emotional state of a person from minimal cues, skills that proved crucial for survival in small-group societies. However, the same cognitive architecture that makes us extraordinarily adept at reading social situations becomes overwhelmed when confronted with multilayered financial instruments whose risks are distributed across time and hidden within legal structures.

When faced with overwhelming complexity, decision-makers revert to heuristics—mental shortcuts that simplify judgments by focusing on salient cues. Enron's management highlighted soaring revenue figures and high trading volumes—visible signs of success—while flouting deeper scrutiny of cash flows and debt levels. Investors and regulators, confronted with daunting technical details, defaulted to surface metrics: quarterly earnings growth, rising stock prices, and prestigious auditors' seals of approval.

The availability heuristic led stakeholders to overweight easily recalled information—Enron's celebrated deals, media praise, and conference presentation highlights—while underweighting harder-to-process data buried in footnotes and technical disclosures. The representativeness heuristic caused investors to assume that Enron's recent success would continue indefinitely, treating short-term performance as representative of long-term prospects.

This reliance on heuristics aligns with "bounded rationality" theories, which acknowledge that individuals make satisficing decisions within cognitive and informational constraints rather than fully optimizing intractable problems. Herbert Simon's groundbreaking work revealed that human decision-making operates under fundamental limitations of attention, memory, and processing capacity that make perfect rationality impossible in complex environments.

**Stress-Induced Tunnel Vision**

Moreover, competitive pressures and performance incentives narrow cognitive bandwidth. Under Skilling's "rank and yank" system, employees knew that failing to meet ambitious targets risked termination. This threat triggered fight-or-flight stress responses, flooding the brain with cortisol and adrenaline—neurochemicals that impair prefrontal cortex functions like analytical reasoning and ethical reflection while enhancing amygdala-driven focus on immediate rewards and survival.

Neuroscientific research on stress and decision-making reveals that chronic stress fundamentally alters brain architecture, shrinking the prefrontal cortex while enlarging the amygdala. This neuroplasticity means that high-stress environments don't just temporarily impair judgment—they can create lasting changes in how individuals process information and make decisions.

In such an environment, sentinel signals that contradicted narratives of success—internal memos about growing liabilities, red-flag audit notes, conservative risk analyses—were subconsciously downregulated to reduce stress, a phenomenon psychologists describe as "motivated reasoning." The human mind's tendency to seek cognitive consistency means that information threatening established beliefs or job security gets filtered out or reinterpreted in ways that preserve psychological equilibrium.

The performance review system at Enron created what cognitive scientists call "goal displacement"—a situation where individuals become so focused on meeting specific metrics that they lose sight of broader organizational purposes. The quarterly performance cycle created artificial time horizons that encouraged short-term optimization at the expense of long-term sustainability, mirroring the way stress responses prioritize immediate survival over future planning.

## Layered Cognitive Distortions

Enron insiders thus experienced layered cognitive distortions: fragmentation of information across organizational silos; heuristic oversimplification by executives, investors, and regulators; and stress-induced tunnel vision within teams. Together, these factors created a perfect storm in which complex fraud could advance unchecked.

The interaction between these different levels of cognitive failure created what complexity theorists call "emergent dysfunction"—systemic problems that arise from the interaction of individually rational behaviors. Each participant in the Enron ecosystem was responding rationally to their immediate incentives and constraints, yet the sum of these rational responses produced catastrophically irrational outcomes.

Reinforcing this dynamic, memetic narratives celebrated Enron's innovation and market leadership, cultivating shared optimism that blinded many to warning signs. The anthropological principle that social norms shape perception explains how collective beliefs—"Enron is invincible"—became self-fulfilling, discouraging individuals from surfacing dissenting data. Cultural narratives function as cognitive filters, making certain types of information more or less salient depending on their fit with prevailing stories about organizational identity and capability.

The phenomenon of "collective narcissism" helps explain how entire organizations can develop unrealistic perceptions of their own capabilities and invulnerability. When success stories become central to organizational identity, contradictory information threatens not just individual careers but the shared narrative that gives meaning to participants' work lives.

## Evolutionary Roots of Corporate Opportunism

Opportunism and amorality at Enron find deep roots in evolutionary drives that once ensured human survival. Anthropological studies of hunter-gatherer societies demonstrate that moral norms were calibrated by survival necessities: sharing food bolstered group cohesion, yet raiding rival camps or hoarding scarce game could secure individual fitness when resources were tight. These ancestral dynamics fostered "moral pragmatism," wherein situational ethics guided behavior—a flexibility that proved adaptive in unpredictable environments.

Archaeological evidence suggests that early human groups practiced complex systems of reciprocal altruism within their bands while maintaining competitive and sometimes aggressive relationships with outside groups. This dual morality—cooperation within the group, competition between groups—created psychological frameworks for contextual ethics that persist in modern organizational life.

In the corporate savanna of 1990s America, executives at Enron perceived deregulated markets as landscapes of scarce and shifting resources, where the ability to exploit every available opening promised competitive advantage. The metaphor of markets as evolutionary landscapes was not merely rhetorical—it reflected genuine psychological processes where ancient survival strategies were activated by competitive pressures and resource uncertainty.

### Cultural Euphemisms and Moral Disengagement

This opportunistic mindset manifested in Enron's leadership culture. Executives like Andrew Fastow and Jeffrey Skilling reframed potentially illicit actions as strategic innovations. Complex off-balance-sheet entities such as LJM and the Raptor partnerships were described internally as "risk management tools," diverting attention from their true function: concealing debt and generating false profitability. Euphemistic labels—"creative financing," "mark-to-market modeling"—served to moralize what were, by any objective standard, deceptive practices.

The power of euphemistic labeling extends beyond simple self-deception to encompass what Albert Bandura identified as "moral disengagement"—psychological mechanisms that allow individuals to behave unethically without experiencing guilt or self-condemnation. By recasting fraudulent activities in positive or neutral terms, Enron's leadership created cognitive frameworks that made unethical behavior psychologically sustainable.

This linguistic reframing echoes insights from philosophical anthropology, which demonstrates that language and narrative shape moral perception: when actions are cloaked in positive terminology, cognitive dissonance is reduced, and ethical boundaries blur. The anthropologist Edward Sapir and linguist Benjamin Lee Whorf argued that language structures thought, and research in moral psychology confirms that the words we use to describe actions influence our ethical evaluations of those actions.

## Regulatory Arbitrage and Market Manipulation

Enron's version of opportunism extended beyond accounting tricks. Trading strategies exploited temporary mismatches in market regulations—so-called "regulatory arbitrage"—where the letter of the law permitted certain transactions even as their substance violated the spirit of fair dealing. For instance, Enron structured virtual trades in California's electricity market during the 2000–2001 crisis that inflated prices without actual supply disruptions, profiting from system vulnerabilities and exacerbating an energy shortage that harmed consumers.

The California energy crisis provides a stark example of how legal opportunism can produce devastating social consequences. Enron traders developed strategies with colorful names like "Fat Boy," "Death Star," and "Get Shorty" that manipulated transmission scheduling and created artificial congestion in power delivery systems. These strategies generated hundreds of millions in profits for Enron while contributing to rolling blackouts and economic disruption that affected millions of Californians.

Investigations by the Federal Energy Regulatory Commission revealed that Enron traders deliberately withheld transmission capacity to drive up costs, illustrating how corporate opportunism can inflict real-world harm when ethical constraints dissolve under profit pressure. Internal emails released during subsequent litigation showed traders celebrating the California crisis and joking about the hardships faced by elderly residents during blackouts, revealing the moral callousness that can emerge when competitive dynamics override human empathy.

**Psychological Mechanisms of Opportunism**

The social and cognitive mechanisms enabling such opportunism are multifaceted. Primal drives for status and resource acquisition remain potent motivators in modern contexts, where material success signals prestige akin to ancestral markers of fitness. Enron's compensation system—heavy stock options and performance bonuses—aligned individual reward structures with short-term financial gains, reinforcing a narrow focus on immediate returns.

Evolutionary psychology research suggests that human status-seeking behaviors evolved in small groups where relative position determined access to mates and resources. In modern corporate environments, these same psychological drives manifest as intense competition for promotions, bonuses, and recognition, often overwhelming more recently evolved capacities for abstract moral reasoning.

Behavioral economists describe this as "present-bias," where near-term benefits are overvalued relative to long-term costs. Executives rationalized speculative ventures and accounting manipulations as acceptable because the future liabilities were discounted or outsourced to offshore SPEs, mirroring the primal impulse to secure immediate resources at the expense of diffuse future consequences.

The psychological concept of "temporal discounting" explains why immediate rewards feel more compelling than future benefits or costs, even when rational analysis would suggest the opposite. This cognitive bias, adaptive in environments where the future was highly uncertain, becomes maladaptive in complex financial systems where current decisions can have catastrophic long-term consequences.

### Cultural Narratives and Heroic Mythology

Moreover, opportunistic morality at Enron was enabled by cultural narratives of entrepreneurial heroism. Business media lionized Skilling and Lay as visionaries who had transformed energy markets through sheer audacity and intellectual flair. These narratives tapped into the archetype of the "self-made man," a motif deeply embedded in American culture since frontier times.

The mythology of American capitalism celebrates figures who break conventional rules to achieve extraordinary success, from nineteenth-century robber barons to twentieth-century technology entrepreneurs. This cultural template provided ready-made justifications for Enron's aggressive practices, framing rule-breaking as evidence of visionary leadership rather than ethical failure.

Philosophical anthropology highlights that mythic narratives shape moral landscapes: when society celebrates risk-taking and market conquest as moral virtues, individuals internalize these values, often overlooking collateral damage or ethical transgressions. At Enron, charismatic leadership and media acclaim created a self-reinforcing loop where aggressive tactics were valorized, dissent was branded as conservatism, and moral skepticism was ostracized as lacking in ambition.

The anthropologist Joseph Campbell's work on the "hero's journey" reveals how cultures use narrative patterns to make sense of individual achievement and moral development. Enron's leadership appropriated heroic narratives while subverting their moral content, creating stories of conquest and transformation that masked predatory behavior.

### Individual Psychology and Rationalization

This confluence of primal drives and cultural exaltation of opportunism elucidates why rational actors within Enron engaged in large-scale deceptions. The moral pragmatism that once fostered adaptive flexibility in foraging bands became pathological in a corporate milieu that conflated innovation with deception. Fastow's secret earnings from SPEs—estimated at $45 million—were rationalized as the rightful fruits of complex deal-making, just as hunters might claim first rights to a prized kill.

The psychological mechanism of "moral licensing" allowed Enron executives to view their innovative financial engineering as earning them permission to bend ethical rules. Having established reputations as creative business leaders, they felt entitled to rewards that others might consider excessive or inappropriate.

Yet unlike ancestral hunts that fed families, Fastow's manipulations drained value from thousands of employees' retirement accounts and undermined entire communities' trust in markets. The divergence between primal justification and societal harm highlights the need for robust ethical frameworks that transcend situational pragmatism.

The scale of harm caused by Enron's collapse—20,000 lost jobs, billions in pension losses, damaged trust in financial markets—illustrates how ancient psychological patterns can produce devastating consequences when applied in complex modern systems without appropriate ethical constraints.

## Tribal Loyalty and Group Cognition

Within the complex social architecture of corporations, group cognition exerts a powerful influence on decision-making, often eclipsing individual moral compasses. At Enron, the social structures of teams and departments functioned analogously to tribal units in small-scale societies: loyalty to the group became a primary identity marker, and conformity to group norms was equated with corporate citizenship.

The evolutionary origins of tribal loyalty trace back millions of years to early hominid groups where survival depended on maintaining cohesive social bonds. Those individuals who developed strong capacities for group loyalty and social conformity were more likely to receive protection and support from their bands, making these traits subject to powerful selective pressures.

Skilling's "rank and yank" performance review system institutionalized competitive tribalism, pitting employees against each other in relentless pursuit of quantitative metrics and reinforcing in-group solidarity at the expense of broader organizational welfare. Anthropologists observe that tribal cohesion fosters rapid collective action and mutual support, adaptive in tight-knit communities facing external threats; yet in corporate settings, this same mechanism can suppress critical inquiry when group norms deviate from ethical standards, as warnings of potential fraud were collectively dismissed to maintain group harmony and performance.

The performance ranking system created what social psychologists call "in-group favoritism" and "out-group derogation"—psychological tendencies to favor members of one's own group while viewing outsiders with suspicion or hostility. Within Enron's high-performing teams, members developed intense loyalty to each other and shared contempt for those who failed to meet aggressive performance standards.

**Cognitive Dissonance and Collective Rationalization**

Cognitive dissonance theory further explains how individuals within these corporate "tribes" reconcile contradictions between their self-image as ethical professionals and their participation in morally dubious practices. Festinger's seminal work outlines that dissonance generates psychological discomfort, which individuals alleviate through rationalization or selective exposure to consonant information.

Leon Festinger's research on cognitive dissonance revealed that humans have a fundamental need for psychological consistency, and when their beliefs and actions conflict, they experience uncomfortable mental tension that motivates efforts to restore balance. This process often involves changing beliefs rather than behaviors, especially when behaviors are locked in by external constraints or social pressures.

At Enron, employees confronted mounting evidence of financial irregularities—whispered concerns about SPEs, late-night risk committee memos, and wary audit comments—but they reduced dissonance by embracing a prevailing narrative: Enron was an innovative pioneer; any red flags were merely teething problems in a revolutionary business model. This collective rationalization was reinforced by organizational rituals—town hall meetings where leadership celebrated record revenues, performance bonuses tied to stock price, and internal communications lauding "creative thinkers."

The social psychology of group dynamics shows that collective rationalization can be even more powerful than individual self-deception. When entire groups share the same cognitive dissonance, they can provide mutual reinforcement for increasingly elaborate rationalizations that would be unsustainable for isolated individuals.

Through repetitive social rituals, the tribe's shared beliefs hardened, sidelining dissent and amplifying dissonance-reducing myths. The anthropological concept of "groupthink," developed by Irving Janis, describes how cohesive groups can develop shared illusions of unanimity and invulnerability that prevent realistic assessment of risks and alternatives.

### Moral Disengagement Mechanisms

Tribal loyalty also facilitated moral disengagement mechanisms identified by Albert Bandura—euphemistic labeling, diffusion of responsibility, and dehumanization of "outsiders" who questioned Enron's practices. Financial engineers described deceptive accounting techniques in neutral or positive terms—"problem-solving vehicles" rather than manipulative traps—obliterating moral connotations. Responsibility for fraudulent trades was diffused across teams: "I only conducted the trade; the structure was pre-approved by the deal desk."

Bandura's theory of moral disengagement identifies eight psychological mechanisms that allow individuals to behave unethically without experiencing guilt: moral justification, euphemistic labeling, advantageous comparison, displacement of responsibility, diffusion of responsibility, distortion of consequences, dehumanization, and attribution of blame. Enron's culture systematically employed all of these mechanisms.

Skeptics external to Enron—journalists, regulators, shareholders—were portrayed as uninformed "bystanders" unable to grasp the company's technical prowess, thereby dehumanizing criticism and bolstering internal solidarity. These psychological defenses mirror those seen in cohesive groups facing existential threats, where moral disengagement enables group members to commit acts contrary to external norms without self-condemnation.

The dehumanization of critics was particularly striking in internal communications, where external analysts who questioned Enron's practices were dismissed with derogatory language that portrayed them as intellectually inferior or motivated by jealousy rather than legitimate concern.

## Ritual, Myth, and Corporate Culture

Anthropological research into ritual and myth provides insight into how corporate cultures promulgate narratives that sustain tribal loyalty. Enron's leadership curated an origin myth: from gas pipelines to digital trading empires, positioning the company as a transformative force in global markets. Such mythic narratives, featuring heroic entrepreneurs and underdog-turned-giant arcs, enchanted employees and investors alike.

The power of organizational mythology extends beyond simple storytelling to encompass what anthropologists call "sacred narratives"—stories that define group identity and provide meaning that transcends individual self-interest. Enron's origin story functioned as a corporate creation myth that gave employees a sense of participating in something historically significant.

In mythic terms, the tribe's founder-figures, Lay and Skilling, were invested with near-mythical authority, their pronouncements treated as revelations rather than strategic communications. The anthropologist Victor Turner's concept of "communitas"—intense experiences of unity emerged during collective rituals—applies to Enron's high-pressure deal closings and investor presentations, where shared adrenaline and cheering crowds deepened tribal bonds and precipitated temporary states of moral euphoria, further silencing critical next-day reflections.

These ritualistic experiences created what Turner called "liminal" states—threshold conditions where normal social rules are suspended and participants experience intense emotional bonding. In Enron's case, these liminal moments occurred during major deal announcements, quarterly earnings releases, and company-wide celebrations of financial milestones.

### The Perils of Whistleblowing

These dynamics elucidate why internal critics like Sherron Watkins found it so perilous to speak up. Whistleblowers breached tribal loyalty and stirred dissonance among peers. Corporate anthropologists note that whistleblowing in tight-knit groups often triggers severe ostracism, as it violates unspoken social contracts. Watkins' 2001 memo to Kenneth Lay warning of an "implosion waiting to happen" was met with defensive anger rather than gratitude, demonstrating the cultural power of tribal bonds. The subsequent marginalization of dissenters sends a chilling message: tribal loyalty and group cohesion supersede individual moral authority.

Research on whistleblowing reveals that individuals who report organizational misconduct face not only formal retaliation but also informal social punishment that can be even more devastating. The anthropologist James Scott's work on "hidden transcripts" shows how subordinated groups develop elaborate ways of expressing dissent without directly challenging authority, but corporate environments often provide no such safe spaces for moral criticism.

The phenomenon of "messenger shooting"—where organizations blame those who bring bad news rather than addressing underlying problems—reflects deep psychological tendencies to preserve group harmony by eliminating sources of cognitive dissonance rather than confronting uncomfortable truths.

**Cultural Valorization and Cognitive Bias Activation**

Modern business behavior emerges at the intersection of organizational culture, ethical frameworks, and cognitive architectures shaped by human evolution. Enron's trajectory demonstrates how misaligned cultures and incentive systems can activate cognitive biases—advantageous heuristics in ancestral contexts—that become destructive in complex corporate environments. This section examines the dynamic interplay among these elements, drawing on interdisciplinary research to propose integrative strategies for promoting ethical, sustainable decision-making.

Cultures define which behaviors are celebrated and which are punished, shaping the salience of cognitive shortcuts. Enron's high-performance culture valorized rapid profit generation, innovative deal creation, and bold risk-taking. Company communications lauded "dealmakers" who closed complex trades that delivered record revenues, while those emphasizing caution or compliance were characterized as "risk-averse" or "not team players."

The cultural emphasis on dealmaking created what anthropologists call "prestige hierarchies"—social ranking systems based on culturally valued achievements. In traditional societies, prestige might be earned through hunting prowess, storytelling ability, or spiritual leadership. At Enron, prestige was measured primarily by deal size and revenue generation, creating powerful incentives for employees to pursue increasingly aggressive strategies.

This valorization aligned seamlessly with evolved human tendencies—such as status striving and in-group signaling—that prioritize actions rewarded by the group. Cognitive biases like overconfidence, status-quo bias, and confirmation bias were thus amplified: executives overestimated their abilities to manage risks, favored information confirming Enron's success narrative, and downplayed contradictory data as anomalies.

The psychology of status competition reveals that individuals will often engage in increasingly risky behaviors to maintain their position in social hierarchies, especially when those hierarchies are based on performance metrics that can be gamed or manipulated. This creates escalating cycles of competitive behavior that can ultimately threaten the entire system.

Behavioral ethics research underscores that culture can serve as a cognitive nudge, steering individuals toward ethical or unethical behavior depending on which cues are made salient. In cultures that highlight honesty and transparency, employees experience moral reminders that activate ethical schemas, counteracting biases toward self-interest. Conversely, cultures emphasizing financial outcomes without moral context trigger reward-focused cognition, where short-term gains overshadow long-term ethical considerations. Enron's culture provided continuous reinforcement—bonuses, promotions, public accolades—for financial performance, creating a cognitive environment where ethical reflection was deprioritized.

**Ethical Frameworks and Evolved Moral Intuitions**

Philosophical debates distinguish between deontological ethics (duty-based), consequentialism (outcomes-based), and virtue ethics (character-based). Each framework interacts differently with human moral intuitions, which evolved to navigate social cooperation within small groups. Moral foundations theory identifies core intuitions—care/harm, fairness/cheating, loyalty/betrayal, authority/subversion, sanctity/degradation—that guide moral judgments.

Jonathan Haidt's research on moral foundations theory reveals that humans possess multiple innate moral sensitivities that evolved to address different challenges of group living. The care/harm foundation responds to suffering and vulnerability; fairness/cheating addresses issues of reciprocity and justice; loyalty/betrayal manages in-group cooperation; authority/subversion deals with hierarchy and leadership; and sanctity/degradation governs concepts of purity and degradation.

Enron's practices systematically violated multiple moral foundations: care was breached through harm to employees; fairness was subverted by insider enrichment; loyalty shifted from stakeholders to narrow in-group alliances; authority was abused by charismatic leaders; and sanctity was degraded by euphemistic redefinitions of fraud as "innovation."

The systematic violation of multiple moral foundations helps explain the intensity of public revulsion toward Enron's practices. When organizations violate just one or two moral foundations, they may maintain support from those who prioritize different values. But Enron's comprehensive moral violations created broad-based condemnation across different moral perspectives.

An integrative ethical framework that aligns with evolved moral intuitions can strengthen resistance to unethical temptations. By embedding moral language that resonates with innate intuitions—highlighting fairness to investors, care for employees' livelihoods, and loyalty to broader societal interests—organizations can activate moral heuristics at decision points. For instance, requiring executives to contemplate the human impact of financial decisions taps into care/harm intuitions, while transparent disclosures reinforce fairness. Enron lacked these moral anchors; instead, its ethical infrastructure hinged solely on compliance checklists, which failed to engage deeper moral cognition and thus proved insufficient when confronted with sophisticated rationalizations.

**Designing Cultures That Harmonize Cognition and Ethics**

Creating organizational cultures that harmonize cognitive structures with ethical imperatives requires intentional design across multiple levels: leadership exemplars, incentive systems, rituals, and structural safeguards. First, leadership must model ethical sensitivity and cognitive humility—acknowledging limitations and fostering environments where questioning is valued. Anthropological studies of successful cooperative groups reveal that leaders who admit error and seek collective input cultivate psychological safety, enabling sentinel signals to surface without fear of reprisal. At Enron, leaders rarely displayed vulnerability; admissions of uncertainty were equated with weakness, reinforcing cognitive overconfidence.

Research on psychological safety, pioneered by Amy Edmondson, shows that team performance is significantly enhanced when members feel safe to voice concerns, admit mistakes, and ask questions without fear of embarrassment or retaliation. This creates environments where sentinel awareness can function effectively, as individuals are willing to share information that might be uncomfortable or challenging to prevailing assumptions.

Second, incentive structures must balance financial performance with ethical behavior. Pay-for-performance systems should incorporate metrics that reflect long-term stakeholder value—employee well-being, customer satisfaction, community impact—thereby channeling reward-focused cognition toward prosocial outcomes. Behavioral economists advocate "balanced scorecards" that include nonfinancial indicators, mitigating present-bias and aligning immediate incentives with sustainable objectives. Enron's hyper-focus on stock price and quarterly earnings triggered short-termism that undermined systemic resilience; balanced incentives could have countered this drift.

The concept of "triple bottom line" accounting—measuring performance in terms of profit, people, and planet—represents one approach to creating more holistic incentive systems. When executive compensation and performance evaluation incorporate social and environmental factors alongside financial metrics, decision-makers are more likely to consider the broader consequences of their actions.

Third, organizational rituals and narratives play a pivotal role in embedding ethics. Regular "ethical huddles," where teams reflect on recent challenges through moral lenses, can reinforce moral schemas and communal accountability. Celebrating cases of principled dissent—whistleblower commendations—and integrating stories of ethical decision-making into onboarding and training create cultural memories of integrity. Anthropologists note that rituals solidify group identity and values; ethical rituals can thus recalibrate tribal loyalty toward organizational ideals rather than narrow performance metrics. Enron's rituals celebrated deal closures but offered no parallel rituals honoring ethical vigilance.

The anthropologist Arnold van Gennep's work on "rites of passage" reveals how rituals can transform individual and group identity. Organizations that create rituals around ethical decision-making—ceremonies recognizing ethical courage, regular storytelling about moral exemplars, collective reflection on ethical dilemmas—can gradually shift cultural values and behavioral norms.

Fourth, structural safeguards must institutionalize cognitive checks to counter biases. Techniques include "premortems" for anticipating failures, red-team audits that challenge prevailing assumptions, and decision-support systems that highlight ethical considerations alongside financial metrics. Technology can facilitate these processes—for example, AI tools that flag unusual transactions for human review, or dashboards that visualize long-term risk exposures. Importantly, these systems must be decentralized, granting whistleblowers and independent units real authority and protection, thereby reinforcing sentinel networks across cognitive and social dimensions.

The concept of "red teaming"—borrowed from military planning—involves creating independent groups whose job is to challenge assumptions and identify weaknesses in proposed strategies. When applied to corporate decision-making, red teams can help identify ethical blind spots and unintended consequences that might not be apparent to those directly involved in planning and implementation.

Interdisciplinary Insights for Sustainable Business Behavior

Synthesizing insights from philosophy, anthropology, psychology, and systems theory reveals that sustainable business behavior emerges when organizations design cultures, structures, and practices that leverage human cognitive strengths while mitigating vulnerabilities. Philosophical ethics provides normative frameworks to articulate shared values; anthropology illuminates how cultures shape moral practices; psychology exposes cognitive biases; and systems theory clarifies feedback loops and emergent patterns. Enron's collapse reflected failures at each level: normative frameworks were limited to compliance; cultural practices valorized opportunism; cognitive biases went unchecked; and systemic fragilities amplified misconduct.

The interdisciplinary approach recognizes that human behavior in organizations cannot be understood through any single lens. Economic models that assume rational decision-making miss the role of emotion and social pressure. Psychological theories that focus on individual cognition neglect cultural and structural factors. Anthropological analyses that emphasize culture may underestimate the power of individual agency and choice.

To build resilient institutions, leaders must embrace interdisciplinary approaches. Governance models should incorporate ethical theory training for executives, anthropological assessments of cultural dynamics, psychological workshops on bias recognition, and systems mapping of organizational interdependencies. Such hybrid programs can foster leaders capable of navigating ethical complexities, recognizing the interplay of primal drives, cultural narratives, and cognitive constraints. Only by addressing the human dimension integrally—combining rules with rituals, structures with stories, and incentives with introspection—can businesses transcend the cycle of fraud and collapse.

The integration of multiple disciplinary perspectives creates what complexity theorists call "requisite variety"—the ability to match the complexity of challenges with correspondingly sophisticated responses. Organizations facing the multifaceted challenges of modern business environments require equally multifaceted approaches to governance and decision-making.

**Combating Tribal Dysfunction Through Structural Reform**

Combating such entrenched group cognition requires both structural and cultural interventions. Structurally, organizations must institute "red-team" functions or independent audit units that operate outside normal tribal hierarchies, empowered to critique and challenge prevailing norms without fear of reprisal. Cognitive scientists advocate "pre-mortem" exercises, where teams imagine a future failure and analyze potential causes, thereby preemptively introducing dissent into group narratives.

The pre-mortem technique, developed by psychologist Gary Klein, involves asking team members to imagine that their project has failed catastrophically and then work backward to identify what might have gone wrong. This approach helps overcome the optimism bias and planning fallacy that often plague group decision-making by making potential problems psychologically salient before they become actual problems.

Culturally, leadership must model vulnerability and openness to contrary viewpoints, normalizing ethical debate as a core ritual rather than an aberration. Incorporating anthropological rituals—such as rotating leadership of ethics committees, communal reflections on past ethical failures, and public celebrations of integrity—can recalibrate tribal loyalty toward collective moral standards rather than narrow performance metrics.

The concept of "distributed leadership" suggests that ethical responsibility should not be concentrated in a few individuals but spread throughout the organization through rotating roles, cross-functional teams, and mechanisms that encourage widespread participation in moral decision-making.

**Addressing Primal Drives Through Cultural Design**

Addressing opportunism rooted in primal survival strategies thus requires integrating structural and cultural interventions. Technological solutions—such as real-time integrated risk platforms—can reduce fragmentation of sentinel awareness, but they cannot eliminate the underlying impulse to exploit system gaps. Organizational cultures must explicitly valorize long-term stewardship and collective welfare, counterbalancing short-term reward biases.

The challenge is to create cultural narratives that make long-term thinking and collective welfare as psychologically compelling as immediate rewards and individual success. This requires understanding how evolutionary psychology shapes motivation and designing cultural systems that align ancient drives with modern ethical imperatives.

Philosophical constructs like virtue ethics, which emphasize character development and habituation of moral dispositions, offer pathways toward embedding integrity into business practices. Anthropological insights suggest that rituals and communal narratives—annual ethics retreats, recognition of employees who report concerns, and storytelling that celebrates principled leadership—can reshape cultural norms, aligning primal drives with prosocial outcomes.

Virtue ethics, tracing back to Aristotle, focuses on the development of good character traits through practice and habituation. Unlike rule-based or outcome-based approaches, virtue ethics recognizes that ethical behavior emerges from ingrained dispositions that are developed through repeated practice in supportive cultural contexts.

**Future Directions and Systemic Integration**

Looking ahead, emerging challenges—digital platforms, climate risks, global supply chain complexities—will intensify pressures on cognitive and ethical systems. Novel business models leveraging AI and algorithmic decision-making introduce new cognitive blind spots, where human oversight may struggle to comprehend opaque machine learning processes. The anthropological imperative for collective vigilance remains critical: cross-disciplinary sentinel networks must evolve to monitor algorithmic risks and ethical implications of technological innovation. Philosophical reflection on the moral status of nonhuman agents and the values embedded in code will become as essential as traditional discussions of corporate governance.

The rise of artificial intelligence and automated decision-making systems creates new challenges for traditional approaches to corporate governance and ethical oversight. When algorithms make decisions based on patterns in data that humans cannot easily interpret, conventional accountability mechanisms may prove inadequate.

The concept of "algorithmic accountability" involves developing new forms of oversight that can address the unique challenges posed by automated systems—their opacity, their potential for bias amplification, their ability to operate at scales and speeds that overwhelm human comprehension.

Enron's story serves as a touchstone for these future challenges. Its lessons underscore that technological sophistication and regulatory reforms, while necessary, are insufficient without cultural and cognitive alignment. The fusion of philosophical and anthropological insights offers a pathway: organizations can harness human evolutionary gifts—social reciprocity, moral intuition, collective learning—while erecting cultural architectures that channel these strengths toward ethical, sustainable outcomes. In doing so, they honor the deeper purpose of business: creating value not only in economic terms but in enhancing human flourishing and societal well-being.

## Conclusion: Integrating Ancient Wisdom with Modern Challenges

In sum, group cognition, cognitive dissonance, and tribal loyalty intertwined at Enron to sustain a culture of collective self-deception. Recognizing these anthropological and psychological structures is essential for designing organizations that balance cohesion with critical inquiry, enabling teams to harness the strengths of tribal bonds—mutual trust, rapid coordination, and shared identity—while safeguarding against moral disengagement and systemic fraud.

The challenge for modern organizations is to preserve the benefits of tribal loyalty—the trust, cooperation, and shared commitment that make collective action possible—while preventing these same mechanisms from becoming tools of self-deception and moral compromise. This requires sophisticated understanding of how human psychology operates in organizational contexts and deliberate design of systems that promote both unity and diversity of thought.

In conclusion, sentinel awareness in its ancestral form provided reliable collective vigilance in small groups confronting immediate threats. Modern corporations, however, require integrated platforms for pooling distributed alerts across functions and empowering rapid, cross-disciplinary responses. Without such systems—and mindful of inherent cognitive biases—organizations remain vulnerable to sophisticated deceptions that prey on fragmented awareness and heuristic shortcuts. Enron's failure thus illustrates the urgent need to redesign corporate sentinel networks, blending technological surveillance with cultural norms that encourage information-sharing and protect dissenters who raise existential alarms.

The path forward requires recognizing that human beings are not merely rational economic actors but complex evolved organisms whose behavior is shaped by deep psychological patterns, cultural narratives, and social structures. Only by understanding and working with these patterns, rather than ignoring or trying to overcome them, can we design organizations that serve both human flourishing and economic prosperity in an increasingly complex and interconnected world.

# Chapter Twelve
## Lessons Learned and Forward Outlook

Preventing another Enron requires a holistic synthesis of insights from multiple disciplines—systems theory, organizational psychology, computer science, and legal studies—to design resilient corporate architectures. At the core lies the principle of redundancy: distributing oversight functions across independent nodes so that no single failure can compromise the whole system. In networked systems theory, redundancy emerges through overlapping controllers and feedback loops; organizationally, this translates into multiple, autonomous audit, risk, and compliance units empowered to cross-check each other.

Concrete pilots illustrate this principle in action. For example, GlobalFoods Inc. deployed overlapping risk committees during a commodity price plunge in 2023—its trading desk, treasury unit, and a newly formed "market intelligence council" all validated counterparty positions independently, via twice-daily reconciliation reports. When one desk flagged unusual credit requests, the others corroborated and escalated the issue within hours, averting a multi-million-dollar exposure and demonstrating how theoretical redundancy translates into rapid detection and response.

Technological solutions enhance these structures. Blockchain's immutable ledgers can serve as distributed "witnesses" to every financial transaction, ensuring transparent audit trails. By recording contracts, SPE formations, and mark-to-market entries on a permissioned blockchain, companies create a permanent, tamper-resistant history that auditors, regulators, and stakeholders can verify independently. Smart contracts—self-executing code on blockchain—can enforce pre-defined compliance rules (e.g., automatically flagging off-balance-sheet transfers exceeding threshold limits) without human intervention.

In practice, a European energy trader trial in late 2024 streamed SPE formation events on a permissioned blockchain. A smart-contract rule required independent third-party capital contributions of at least 20 percent within 48 hours. Transactions failing to meet this criterion were automatically suspended and alerted to the compliance desk. Over six months, the trial detected and halted seven unauthorized offshore partnerships—an early test of how code-based enforcement can close loopholes faster than traditional legal reviews.

These mechanisms align with anthropological insights: just as communal memory safeguards tribal norms through storytelling and ritual, blockchain preserves corporate memory through cryptographic consensus, preventing information fragmentation and enabling real-time sentinel awareness.

Artificial intelligence (AI) offers complementary capabilities. Machine-learning algorithms can analyze vast streams of transactional and communications data to detect anomalous patterns—unusually large round-trip trades, sudden creation of new SPEs, or clusters of related-party transactions. Natural language processing can scan emails, memos, and meeting transcripts for euphemistic terms ("creative financing," "special purpose") that historically preceded fraud. By continuously updating risk models with human feedback, AI systems can adapt to evolving schemes, functioning as proactive guardians rather than reactive auditors.

In a 2022 financial-services pilot, an AI model flagged 92 percent of known fraud cases but produced a 17 percent false-positive rate. Human auditors found many alerts involved legitimate mergers and divestitures using novel legal language—highlighting the need for explainable AI. The firm then layered rule-based filters on top of black-box outputs to contextualize alerts by transaction purpose codes, reducing noise and preserving human trust in automated monitoring.

However, AI itself must be governed: opaque "black-box" models risk replicating biases, and adversarial actors may intentionally obfuscate communications. Thus, transparency and interpretability in AI design are essential, mirroring philosophical demands for accountable reason giving and enabling human overseers to understand why certain alerts are raised.

Decentralized accountability frameworks further bolster systemic resilience. Inspired by blockchain governance models, organizations can adopt stakeholder DAO (Decentralized Autonomous Organization) structures where employees, external auditors, and even public interest representatives hold tokenized voting rights on major financial decisions. Such DAOs distribute decision-making power, reducing concentrated authority that enabled Enron's leadership to override internal objections.

Yet implementing DAOs in traditional corporations faces legal hurdles. Under U.S. securities law, tokens granting voting rights may constitute transferable securities, triggering registration requirements. In 2023, a mid-cap tech firm's DAO pilot was paused when its pilot tokens fell under state Blue Sky statutes. The firm subsequently engaged regulators through a regtech sandbox, co-developing a hybrid model using restricted-use tokens exempt from security registration. This real-life adjustment underscores the importance of legal-policy collaboration when adapting DAO governance.

Balancing innovation, ethics, and governance demands careful calibration of incentive systems. Token-based reward mechanisms can align individual contributions to ethical outcomes: for example, issuing "integrity tokens" to employees who identify genuine risks or propose compliance improvements, redeemable for professional development opportunities or bonus multipliers.

In a 2021 experiment at FinTrust Bank, employees received "ethics points" redeemable for paid training days when reporting potential compliance issues. Over 18 months, reported near-misses rose by 230 percent, and actual compliance violations fell by 45 percent. Surveys indicated that the token system reframed whistleblowing as a recognized contribution rather than a risky act—validating gamification as a lever for ethical culture change.

Regulatory interfaces must evolve alongside corporate innovations. Standard-setting bodies—such as the Financial Accounting Standards Board and international counterparts—should develop protocols for digital assets, smart-contract audits, and AI-based risk monitoring, ensuring interoperability across jurisdictions. Collaborative "regtech sandboxes" can allow firms and regulators to pilot cutting-edge solutions in controlled environments, refining policies before broad deployment. These sandboxes embody the anthropological practice of safe-to-fail experiments, where small-scale trials inform larger systemic transformations.

Singapore's 2022 RegLab sandbox offers a model: it enabled a consortium of banks and fintech firms to trial a shared KYC blockchain, with MAS providing oversight and temporary regulatory relief. The pilot produced a 40 percent reduction in onboarding times while retaining strict anti-money-laundering controls via real-time regulator dashboards. Such public-private experimentation demonstrates how anthropological safe-to-fail principles can accelerate innovation while protecting systemic stability.

Finally, embedding ethical reflection into technological design is crucial. The emerging field of ethical AI emphasizes value-sensitive design: integrating stakeholder values into algorithms from inception rather than retrofitting controls. Similarly, "blockchain ethics" calls for transparency about consensus mechanisms, governance rules, and data privacy.

In the 2023 Ethereum Foundation Ethics Review, community members debated the social impact of moving to proof-of-stake. Transparency around validator incentives, stake concentration, and on-chain governance proposals became central ethical questions—mirroring corporate debates over stakeholder representation in DAOs. This example from public-blockchain governance highlights how ethical design principles developed in decentralized networks can inform private-sector blockchain ethics frameworks.

By foregrounding ethical considerations, organizations avoid technological determinism—the belief that code alone can enforce morality—and instead cultivate cultures where technology amplifies human responsibility rather than replacing it.

In sum, systemic and technological solutions to the Enron legacy require interweaving redundant oversight structures, blockchain-based transparency, AI-driven anomaly detection, decentralized governance, incentive realignment, regulatory collaboration, and ethical design. This integrated approach transforms corporate architecture into a resilient living system—one capable of detecting emergent threats, learning from near-misses, and aligning human cognition with ethical imperatives—thereby minimizing the likelihood of future corporate catastrophes.

A complementary field trial in 2023 used zero-knowledge proofs to verify collateral ratios in a syndicated loan without disclosing borrower data. Regulators received cryptographic confirmation of compliance, while commercial sensitivities remained protected. This proof-of-concept illustrates how emerging cryptographic tools can extend transparency without compromising confidentiality—an essential capability for future regulatory-technology integration.

Emerging technologies offer powerful tools to detect, prevent, and deter corporate misconduct. Artificial intelligence (AI), blockchain, and decentralized governance models each address distinct vulnerabilities revealed by the Enron case, and when integrated, can create layered defenses against systemic fraud.

AI's strength lies in pattern recognition at scale. Supervised machine-learning algorithms trained on historical data can identify anomalous financial transactions—such as unusual spikes in round-trip trading or rapid SPE formations—flagging them for human review. Unsupervised learning techniques, including clustering and anomaly detection, uncover hidden correlations among counterparty networks or off–balance-sheet vehicles that standard audits may overlook. Natural language processing (NLP) further enhances oversight by scanning vast corpora of internal communications for euphemistic or emotionally charged language associated with unethical conduct. For example, NLP models can surface memos containing code words like "special purpose" or "creative modeling" that historically signaled deceit. Integrating AI with human expertise ensures continuous learning and adaptation: as new deception schemes emerge, feedback loops retrain models, improving future detection.

Blockchain provides immutable record-keeping and decentralization. By recording all corporate financial transactions—asset transfers, SPE creations, debt issuances—on a permissioned blockchain, organizations establish a cryptographically secure ledger that resists tampering. Auditors and regulators access this shared ledger to verify transaction histories in real time, eliminating reliance on management-generated reports. Smart contracts automate compliance: code enforces covenants (for example, preventing SPE formation without independent capital contributions) and triggers alerts when predefined thresholds are breached. This "code-as-law" approach embeds governance rules into transaction execution, reducing opportunities for human override.

Decentralized accountability extends blockchain's principles to corporate governance. Decentralized Autonomous Organizations (DAOs) leverage token-based voting systems to distribute decision-making authority among stakeholders—employees, external auditors, board members, and even public interest representatives. Tokens represent voting weight or "reputation stakes" earned through contributions to risk management or compliance. Major corporate actions—such as approving new structured finance transactions—require a quorum of token holders to vote, ensuring that no single executive can unilaterally bypass controls. DAO frameworks foster transparency by publishing voting records, debates, and rationale on-chain, creating an auditable trail of governance decisions.

These technologies must be supported by ethical AI design and governance protocols. AI models should be interpretable, with explainable outputs that allow auditors to understand why a transaction was flagged. Blockchain governance requires clear on-chain rules, defined upgrade mechanisms, and dispute resolution processes to adapt to evolving regulatory and business needs. Token-based voting must guard against concentration of power, for instance by capping individual token holdings or implementing quadratic voting to prevent plutocratic control.

Technological innovation accelerates business capabilities but also introduces novel risks. Balancing innovation with ethical governance requires integrated frameworks that align technical advances with human values and oversight mechanisms.

A key principle is risk-informed innovation—pursuing new technologies while systematically assessing and mitigating potential harms. Prior to deploying AI or blockchain solutions, organizations should conduct impact assessments that evaluate risks to data privacy, algorithmic bias, governance vulnerabilities, and unintended market effects. Multidisciplinary teams—comprising technologists, ethicists, legal experts, and frontline employees—collaborate to identify scenarios where technology could be misused or create new blind spots. These assessments inform design choices, such as data governance policies, model transparency requirements, and layered authentication controls.

Ethical guidelines for emerging technologies can be codified in technology stewardship charters. Such charters articulate organizational commitments—to fairness, accountability, transparency, and human agency—and set thresholds for acceptable system behaviors.

For AI, stewardship includes human-in-the-loop controls for high--risk decisions, periodic algorithmic audits, and redress protocols for flagged individuals or transactions. For blockchain, charters define governance councils to oversee protocol upgrades, token distribution principles, and mechanisms for resolving on-chain disputes. Technology stewardship institutionalizes ethical reflection alongside technical development, embedding values into the innovation lifecycle.

Governance frameworks must adapt to distributed technologies. Traditional board structures may lack expertise to oversee AI models or blockchain protocols. Organizations should establish dedicated technology oversight committees with cross-functional membership—data scientists, compliance officers, external advisors—to review technical risk reports, audit findings, and governance metrics. These committees meet quarterly (at minimum) and maintain real-time dashboards tracking key risk indicators—AI model drift, smart-contract exceptions, on-chain governance votes—to ensure proactive oversight.

The integration of systemic and technological solutions demands holistic strategies anchored in interdisciplinary principles:

Redundant sentinel networks: Overlay human oversight (internal audit, ethics helplines) with technological sentinels (AI monitoring, blockchain alerts) to ensure no single node's failure compromises detection.

Distributed governance: Combine centralized leadership for strategy with decentralized accountability for oversight—using DAOs and token-based voting to democratize governance without sacrificing efficiency.

Ethical design and reflexivity: Embed moral deliberation in technology development through stewardship charters, cross-disciplinary impact assessments, and continuous ethical training.

Cultural alignment: Cultivate organizational narratives celebrating transparency, whistleblowing, and long-term value creation; integrate ethical rituals (e.g., annual ethics audits, red team reviews) into corporate calendars.

Regulatory collaboration: Engage regulators in regtech sandboxes to co-develop standards for AI and blockchain in financial reporting, ensuring interoperability and legal compliance across jurisdictions.

Continuous learning: Treat organizational risk management as an adaptive system—analyzing past near-misses, updating sentinel protocols, and evolving governance charters in response to new threats.

Looking forward, advanced AI techniques—such as federated learning—can enable collaborative fraud detection across firms and industries without compromising data privacy. Decentralized identity solutions can authenticate individuals participating in governance votes, reducing sybil attacks in DAOs. Emerging technologies in zero-knowledge proofs offer ways to verify compliance (e.g., capital adequacy, reserve requirements) without revealing proprietary details. Each innovation expands the toolkit for resilient corporate architectures, yet also underscores the imperative for interdisciplinary stewardship.

The convergence of systems theory, cognitive science, anthropology, and philosophy provides a robust foundation for these innovations. By acknowledging human cognitive limitations, primal drives, group dynamics, and ethical imperatives, organizations can design integrated solutions that harness technology while safeguarding trust. The Enron collapse stands as a somber reminder of what can occur when human ingenuity outpaces ethical and governance frameworks. In response, a future corporate landscape fortified by systemic redundancy, technological transparency, and values-centered governance offers hope that the lessons of Enron will guide, rather than haunt, the next generation of business innovation

## Concise Timeline of Key Events and Reforms

1992 – Energy Policy Act partially deregulates wholesale electricity markets, enabling energy trading platforms.

1995 – Private Securities Litigation Reform Act raises pleading standards for securities fraud and grants safe harbor for forward-looking statements.

1996 – Telecommunications Act removes barriers to entry, spurring aggressive competition and corporate expansion.

1997 – Nick Szabo publishes "Formalizing and Securing Relationships on Public Networks," laying groundwork for smart contracts.

1998 – Enron launches its first broadband trading unit, foreshadowing financialization of non-energy assets.

2000 – Enron Raptor SPEs created to conceal debt; FERC begins investigating California "energy crisis" manipulations.

October 16, 2001 – Wall Street Journal front-page exposé questions Enron's SPE use, triggering stock price collapse.

November 8, 2001 – Enron restates four years of earnings, admitting $586 million in overstatements.

November 15, 2001 – Enron files Chapter 11 bankruptcy, citing $63.4 billion assets and $13.2 billion debt.

January 2002 – Congressional hearings unveil systemic regulatory and board failures; Sherron Watkins testifies on whistleblower risks.

July 24, 2002 – Congress enacts Sarbanes-Oxley Act, establishing PCAOB, CEO/CFO certification, and enhanced internal control reporting.

2004 – SEC's PCAOB fully operational; FERC tightens energy derivatives reporting and enforcement.

2008 – Nakamoto publishes Bitcoin white paper, introducing permissionless blockchain and distributed consensus.

2009 – Dodd-Frank Act mandates enhanced derivatives oversight, swap-push-out rules, and whistleblower incentives at SEC.

2013 – Floridi's The Ethics of Information highlights value-sensitive design in digital systems.

2014 – Ethereum white paper formalizes decentralized application platforms and programmable smart contracts.

2016 – Tapscott & Tapscott's Blockchain Revolution articulates blockchain's potential for transparent corporate governance.

2017 – Bandura's studies on moral disengagement inform organizational ethics training programs.

2019 – Jobin, Ienca & Vayena map global AI ethics guidelines, emphasizing explainability and accountability.

2020 – Gartner's Magic Quadrant identifies mature AI/ML platforms for risk monitoring and anomaly detection.

2022 – ESG reporting standards proliferate; stakeholder DAOs pilot token-based governance in select enterprises.

2025 – RegTech sandboxes launched in EU and US, enabling co-development of AI-driven audit and blockchain compliance trials.

# About the Author

Allen Schery stands as a singular voice at the intersection of history, anthropology, sports scholarship, and public culture—an author whose commitment to asking big questions has earned him recognition in both academic and popular circles. Born and raised in Brooklyn within sight of Ebbets Field, his earliest memories are inseparable from the roar of the crowd and the mythic aura of the Brooklyn Dodgers. Schery's childhood experiences meeting legends like Jackie Robinson, Roy Campanella, and Duke Snider ignited a passion for sport as living history and seeded a lifelong pursuit of cultural storytelling.

An accomplished Philosophical Anthropologist and Archaeologist who excavated ruins at Chichen Itza Schery's scholarly pursuits took him far from Brooklyn—to Mexico's Yucatán Peninsula, where he engaged in excavation and cultural interpretation, and later to exploring the Dogon Culture who lived in highlands of West Africa and also Mexico's indigenous territories, particularly the Tepehuan people delving into the intricate web of belief, ritual, and social organization. This broad, humanistic lens informs his writing and museum work. As a designer and curator, he transformed the Corvette Americana Museum in Cooperstown, NY, into a landmark of immersive exhibition, lauded for its blend of narrative drama and historical acumen, and continues to bring a curatorial eye to the preservation of sports and social history.

Schery is the founder and principal author of Brooklyn Bridge Books, publishing a diverse and influential catalog. His major works on baseball include "The Boys of Spring: The Birth of the Dodgers," an expansive cultural history of the team's Brooklyn era, and "The Brooklyn Dodgers at Ebbets Field 1913–1957," a lush chronicle of the team's life at one of America's most storied ballparks. "Ebbets to Paradise: O'Malley's Journey to the Coliseum and Dodger Stadium" examines the emotional and civic challenges of the Dodgers' move to the West Coast. In "Corvette Americana: A Cultural Time Tunnel," Schery captures the pulse of American innovation, using the revered automobile as a lens through which to view societal change.

His restless intellectual energy has produced acclaimed works in other domains: "The Mystery of the Ark" blends archaeology and religious imagination, "The Pattern Seeking Ape" and "The Primate Principle" investigate psychology, symbolism, and human evolution, while "Shattered Cross: The Rise, Fall and Undying Legacy of the Knights Templars" and "Illuminati: The Conspiracy that

Never Died" confront the roots of belief, secrecy, and mythmaking. "Sanctity and Shadows – The Unholy See" delves into the contested histories at the heart of the Vatican. "Philosophy is a Human Mind Painting" and "Religion as a Mind Painting" offer provocative and original perspectives on the creation of meaning in human life.

A proud member of the Society for American Baseball Research and an innovator in the curation of immersive museum exhibits, Allen Schery's expertise draws on his meticulous private archive, which includes one of the world's largest collections of Dodgers memorabilia, as well as his belief in the transformative power of narrative. For Schery, history is not merely the past; it is a living force that shapes contemporary identity and imagination.

Currently residing in Southern California, where he continues to write, collect artifacts, and advise cultural institutions, Schery divides his time between research, public speaking, and restoring the connections between collective memory, heritage, and the ongoing drama of American life. Across all his projects, he is a steadfast advocate for thoughtful preservation, intellectual rigor, and the joy of rediscovery—inviting readers and audiences to see themselves reflected in the ever-evolving story of sport, culture, and humanity.

# *Bibliography*

Schery, Allen. The Pattern Seeking Ape: Interdisciplinary Perspectives on Human Cognition and Culture. Brooklyn Bridge Books, 2025.

Schery, Allen. The Primate Principle: Brooklyn Bridge Books, 2025.

Appiah, Kwame Anthony. Cosmopolitanism: Ethics in a World of Strangers. W.W. Norton & Company, 2006.

Boehm, Christopher. Hierarchy in the Forest: The Evolution of Egalitarian Behavior. Harvard University Press, 1999.

de Waal, Frans. Chimpanzee Politics: Power and Sex among Apes. Johns Hopkins University Press, 2007.

de Waal, Frans. Good Natured: The Origins of Right and Wrong in Humans and Other Animals. Harvard University Press, 1996.

Lee, Richard B. The Dobe Ju/'hoansi. 4th ed., Cengage Learning, 2013.

Nisbett, Richard E., and Dov Cohen. Culture of Honor: The Psychology of Violence in the South. Westview Press, 1996.

Nussbaum, Martha C. Frontiers of Justice: Disability, Nationality, Species Membership. Harvard University Press, 2006.

Rawls, John. Political Liberalism. Expanded ed., Columbia University Press, 2005.

Tomasello, Michael. A Natural History of Human Morality. Harvard University Press, 2016.

Whiten, Andrew, et al. "Cultures in Chimpanzees." Nature, vol. 399, no. 6737, 1999, pp. 682–685.

Chapter One

"Blind Faith: How Deregulation and Enron's Influence Over Government Looted Billions from Americans." Public Citizen, Dec. 2001, https://www.citizen.org/wp-content/uploads/blind_faith.pdf.

"Cognitive Dissonance: The Upside of Unease." Corporate Compliance Insights, 19 July 2020, https://www.corporatecomplianceinsights.com/cognitive-dissonance-upside-unease/.

"Cognitive Dissonance in Business: Symptoms, Mitigation and Lessons." LinkedIn, 13 Apr. 2023, https://www.linkedin.com/pulse/cognitive-dissonance-business-symptoms-mitigation-lessons-naman-soni.

Coffee, John C., Jr. "What Caused Enron? A Capsule Social and Economic History of the 1990s." Columbia Law School, 2003, https://scholarship.law.columbia.edu/cgi/viewcontent.cgi?params=

%2Fcontext%2Ffaculty_scholarship%2Farticle%2F5264%2F&path_info=Coffee_What_Caused_Enron.pdf.

"Enron: Not Accounting for the Future." Harbert College of Business, Auburn University, https://harbert.auburn.edu/binaries/documents/center-for-ethical-organizational-cultures/cases/enron.pdf.

"Enron scandal." Encyclopædia Britannica, 25 Sept. 2025, https://www.britannica.com/event/Enron-scandal.

"Enron Scandal and Accounting Fraud: What Happened?" Investopedia, 2 Dec. 2024, https://www.investopedia.com/updates/enron-scandal-summary/.

"Enron scandal." Wikipedia, 5 Feb. 2004, https://en.wikipedia.org/wiki/Enron_scandal.

"Enron's Contribution to the Vitality of Corporate Compliance." Harvard Law School Forum on Corporate Governance, 3 Jan. 2022, https://corpgov.law.harvard.edu/2022/01/03/enrons-contribution-to-the-vitality-of-corporate-compliance/.

"Enron's deregulation fight." Center for Public Integrity, 7 Jan. 2022, http://publicintegrity.org/politics/enrons-deregulation-fight/.

"From Principles to Politics: How Ethics Have Evolved from the 1990s." LinkedIn, 22 May 2025, https://www.linkedin.com/pulse/from-principles-politics-how-ethics-have-evolved-1990s-bill-michels-zgdcc.

"How Have Business Ethics Evolved Over Time?" Investopedia, 20 Mar. 2025, https://www.investopedia.com/ask/answers/022615/how-have-business-ethics-evolved-over-time.asp.

"Innovation Corrupted: How Managers Can Avoid Another Enron." Harvard Business School Working Knowledge, 6 July 2008, https://www.library.hbs.edu/working-knowledge/innovation-corrupted-how-managers-can-avoid-another-enron.

"Management Controls: The Organizational Fraud Triangle of Leadership, Culture and Control in Enron." Ivey Business Journal, 23 Feb. 2015, https://iveybusinessjournal.com/publication/management-controls-the-organizational-fraud-triangle-of-leadership-culture-and-control-in-enron/.

"Revisiting Moral Hazard." The New York Times, 23 Sept. 2008, https://archive.nytimes.com/economix.blogs.nytimes.com/2008/09/24/revisiting-moral-hazard/.

Schery, Allen. The Pattern Seeking Ape: Interdisciplinary Perspectives on Human Cognition and Culture. Brooklyn Bridge Books, 2025.

"The Dark Pattern of Corporate Scandals (Part One)." Ethics Unwrapped, University of Texas at Austin, 29 July 2025, https://ethicsunwrapped.utexas.edu/the-dark-pattern-of-corporate-scandals-part-one.

"The dynamic duo of cognitive dissonance and moral disengagement." ACFE Fraud Magazine, 31 Mar. 2017, https://www.acfe.com/fraud-magazine/all-issues/issue/article?s=2017-april-cognitive-dissonance.

"The Rise and Fall of Enron." Journal of Accountancy, 31 Mar. 2002, https://www.journalofaccountancy.com/issues/2002/apr/theriseandfallofenron/.

"The Value of Corporate Culture." Kellogg School of Management, Northwestern University, https://www.kellogg.northwestern.edu/faculty/sapienza/htm/CorporateCulture.pdf.

"Twenty Years Later: The Lasting Lessons of Enron." Harvard Law School Forum on Corporate Governance, 5 Apr. 2021, https://corpgov.law.harvard.edu/2021/04/05/twenty-years-later-the-lasting-lessons-of-enron/.

"What Really Went Wrong with Enron? A Culture of Evil?" Markkula Center for Applied Ethics, Santa Clara University, 4 Mar. 2002, https://www.scu.edu/ethics/focus-areas/business-ethics/resources/what-really-went-wrong-with-enron/.

"What the 1990s taught us about abusive work environments." New Workplace, 27 May 2012, https://newworkplace.wordpress.com/2012/05/28/what-the-1990s-taught-us-about-abusive-work-environments/.

"When Managers Set Unrealistic Expectations, Employees Cut Ethical Corners." Harvard Business School Working Knowledge, 29 Apr. 2024, https://www.library.hbs.edu/working-knowledge/when-managers-set-unrealistic-expectations-employees-cut-ethical-corners.

---

Chapter Two

"A year ago, Enron Corp. CEO Jeffrey Skilling." UCLA Anderson School of Management, 2002, https://www.anderson.ucla.edu/documents/areas/adm/loeb/02g6-3.pdf.

"Empire of Deceit: Enron's Strategic Moves to Dominate the Energy Market." Enron.net, 31 Dec. 2000, https://enron.net/building-the-empire.

"Enron: Not Accounting for the Future." Harbert College of Business, Auburn University, https://harbert.auburn.edu/binaries/documents/center-for-ethical-organizational-cultures/cases/enron.pdf.

"Enron scandal." Encyclopædia Britannica, 25 Sept. 2025, https://www.britannica.com/event/Enron-scandal.

"Enron Scandal and Accounting Fraud: What Happened?" Investopedia, 2 Dec. 2024, https://www.investopedia.com/updates/enron-scandal-summary/.

"Enron scandal." Wikipedia, 5 Feb. 2004, https://en.wikipedia.org/wiki/Enron_scandal.

"Enron's Skilling Is Sentenced to 24 Years." The New York Times, 23 Oct. 2006, https://www.nytimes.com/2006/10/24/business/24enron.html.

"Former Enron CEO Jeffrey Skilling wants back into the energy business." CNBC, 22 Mar. 2019, https://www.cnbc.com/2019/03/23/former-enron-ceo-jeffrey-skilling-wants-back-into-the-energy-business.html.

"Jeffrey Skilling: Puppet Master of Enron's Entangled Web." Enron.net, 31 Dec. 2005, https://enron.net/jeffrey-skilling-the-mastermind.

"Jeffrey Skilling, Former Enron CEO and Chief Operating Officer." VPM, 4 Apr. 2006, https://www.vpm.org/npr-news/2006-04-05/jeffrey-skilling-former-enron-ceo-and-chief-operating-officer.

"Ken Lay: Enron Founder and CEO's Gigantic Failure." Shortform Books, 12 Aug. 2020, https://www.shortform.com/blog/ken-lay-enron/.

"Ken Lay: The Charismatic Architect - The Enron Saga." Enron.net, 1 Dec. 2001, https://enron.net/ken-lay-the-charismatic-leader.

"Kenneth Lay." Research Starters, EBSCO, 4 July 2006, https://www.ebsco.com/research-starters/biography/kenneth-lay.

"Kenneth Lay: Founding Enron Whose Revenue Was Over $101 Billion." YouTube, 10 Oct. 2022, https://www.youtube.com/watch?v=XkvDUaQK2v0.

"Management Controls: The Organizational Fraud Triangle of Leadership, Culture and Control in Enron." Ivey Business Journal, 23 Feb. 2015, https://iveybusinessjournal.com/publication/management-controls-the-organizational-fraud-triangle-of-leadership-culture-and-control-in-enron/.

Schery, Allen. The Pattern Seeking Ape: Interdisciplinary Perspectives on Human Cognition and Culture. Brooklyn Bridge Books, 2025.

Schery, Allen. Chimpanzee Politics and Moral Cognition: Philosophical Anthropology in Practice. Brooklyn Bridge Books, 2025.

"The dynamic duo of cognitive dissonance and moral disengagement." ACFE Fraud Magazine, 31 Mar. 2017, https://www.acfe.com/fraud-magazine/all-issues/issue/article?s=2017-april-cognitive-dissonance.

"The Enron Trial: A Chronology." Famous Trials, 22 Jan. 2002, https://famous-trials.com/enron/1789-chronology.

"The Mighty Men: Enron." The Flaw, 14 Oct. 2023, https://theflaw.org/articles/the-mighty-men-enron/.

"Timeline: Ken Lay and the Arc of Enron." NPR, 5 July 2006, https://www.npr.org/2006/07/05/5535821/timeline-ken-lay-and-the-arc-of-enron.

"Twenty Years Later: The Lasting Lessons of Enron." Harvard Law School Forum on Corporate Governance, 5 Apr. 2021, https://corpgov.law.harvard.edu/2021/04/05/twenty-years-later-the-lasting-lessons-of-enron/.

"What Really Went Wrong with Enron? A Culture of Evil?" Markkula Center for Applied Ethics, Santa Clara University, 4 Mar. 2002, https://www.scu.edu/ethics/focus-areas/business-ethics/resources/what-really-went-wrong-with-enron/.

Chapter Three

"Arthur Andersen: An Accounting Confidence Crisis." Harbert College of Business, Auburn University, https://harbert.auburn.edu/binaries/documents/center-for-ethical-organizational-cultures/cases/arthur-anderson.pdf.

"Arthur Andersen." Encyclopædia Britannica, 31 Dec. 2024, https://www.britannica.com/money/Arthur-Andersen.

"Arthur Andersen." Wikipedia, 24 Feb. 2002, https://en.wikipedia.org/wiki/Arthur_Andersen.

"BYU study: 20 years later, accountants burned by Enron scandal outperform peers." BYU News, 15 Mar. 2022, https://news.byu.edu/byu-study-20-years-later-accountants-burned-by-enron-scandal-outperform-peers.

"Complaint: SEC v. Andrew S. Fastow." SEC.gov, 9 Feb. 2002, https://www.sec.gov/litigation/complaints/comp17762.htm.

"Enron." FBI, 18 May 2016, https://www.fbi.gov/history/famous-cases/enron.

"Enron and Arthur Andersen: The Case of the Crooked E and the Fallen A." Western Carolina University, https://www.wcu.edu/gpa e/Vol3/Enron%20and%20Aurhur%20Andersen.pdf.

"Enron scandal." Wikipedia, 5 Feb. 2004, https://en.wikipedia.org/wiki/Enron_scandal.

"Enron's Contribution to the Vitality of Corporate Compliance." Harvard Law School Forum on Corporate Governance, 2 Jan. 2022, https://corpgov.law.harvard.edu/2022/01/03/enrons-contribution-to-the-vitality-of-corporate-compliance/.

"Enron whistleblower shares lessons on corporate integrity." UNC Kenan-Flagler Business School, 24 Nov. 2015, https://www.kenan-flagler.unc.edu/news/enron-whistleblower-shares-lessons-on-corporate-integrity/.

"Former Enron Chief Financial Officer Andrew Fastow Pleads Guilty to Conspiracy to Commit Securities and Wire Fraud." FBI, 13 Jan. 2004, https://www.fbi.gov/news/pressrel/press-releases/former-enron-chief-financial-officer-andrew-fastow-pleads-guilty-to-conspiracy-to-commit-securities-and-wire-fraud.

"Former Enron Chief Financial Officer Andrew S. Fastow Charged with Conspiracy, Wire Fraud, Money Laundering, Conflict of Interest." U.S. Department of Justice, 30 Oct. 2002, https://www.justice.gov/archive/opa/pr/2002/October/02_crm_627.htm.

"Jeffrey Skilling, Former Enron CEO and Chief Operating Officer." VPM, 4 Apr. 2006, https://www.vpm.org/npr-news/2006-04-05/jeffrey-skilling-former-enron-ceo-and-chief-operating-officer.

"Jeffrey Skilling: Puppet Master of Enron's Entangled Web." Enron.net, 31 Dec. 2005, https://enron.net/jeffrey-skilling-the-mastermind.

"Ken Lay: The Charismatic Architect - The Enron Saga." Enron.net, 1 Dec. 2001, https://enron.net/ken-lay-the-charismatic-leader.

"Management Controls: The Organizational Fraud Triangle of Leadership, Culture and Control in Enron." Ivey Business Journal, 23 Feb. 2015, https://iveybusinessjournal.com/publication/management-controls-the-organizational-fraud-triangle-of-leadership-culture-and-control-in-enron/.

"Portraits in Oversight: Congress and the Enron Scandal." Carl Levin Center, 17 Mar. 2025, https://sitemap.carllevincenter.com/what-is-oversight/portraits/congress-and-the-enron-scandal/.

"The Enron Collapse: Compliance Failures and Lessons." Planet Compliance, 27 Apr. 2025, https://www.planetcompliance.com/soc-2/enron-collapse-compliance/.

"The Enron Trial: A Chronology." Famous Trials, 22 Jan. 2002, https://famous-trials.com/enron/1789-chronology.

"Timeline: Ken Lay and the Arc of Enron." NPR, 5 July 2006, https://www.npr.org/2006/07/05/5535821/timeline-ken-lay-and-the-arc-of-enron.

"Twenty years later, could another Enron happen?" Association of Certified Fraud Examiners, 31 Oct. 2021, https://www.acfe.com/fraud-magazine/all-issues/issue/article?s=2021-novdec-enron-whistleblower-20-years-later.

"What Really Went Wrong with Enron? A Culture of Evil?" Markkula Center for Applied Ethics, Santa Clara University, 4 Mar. 2002, https://www.scu.edu/ethics/focus-areas/business-ethics/resources/what-really-went-wrong-with-enron/.

"Whistleblowers Should Avoid Internal Reporting Channels." Whistleblowers.org, 18 Apr. 2021, https://www.whistleblowers.org/internal-reporting-channels/.

Chapter Four

"Energy Trader Admits Faking Transactions." The New York Times, 14 May 2002, https://www.nytimes.com/2002/05/14/business/energy-trader-admits-faking-transactions.html.

"Enron: An Accounting Scandal That Changed Everything." Encoursa, 1 May 2023, https://encoursa.com/blog/zp3wpy26/enron-an-accounting-scandal-that-changed-everything.

"Enron: Not Accounting for the Future." Harbert College of Business, Auburn University, https://harbert.auburn.edu/binaries/documents/center-for-ethical-organizational-cultures/cases/enron.pdf.

"Enron and Arthur Andersen: The Case of the Crooked E and the Fallen A." Western Carolina University, https://www.wcu.edu/gpae/Vol3/Enron%20and%20Aurhur%20Andersen.pdf.

"Enron." FBI, 18 May 2016, https://www.fbi.gov/history/famous-cases/enron.

"Enron Scandal - Overview, Role of MTM, Agency Conflicts." Corporate Finance Institute, 5 Oct. 2023, https://corporatefinanceinstitute.com/resources/esg/enron-scandal/.

"Enron scandal." Encyclopædia Britannica, 25 Sept. 2025, https://www.britannica.com/event/Enron-scandal.

"Enron Scandal and Accounting Fraud: What Happened?" Investopedia, 2 Dec. 2024, https://www.investopedia.com/updates/enron-scandal-summary/.

"Enron scandal." Wikipedia, 5 Feb. 2004, https://en.wikipedia.org/wiki/Enron_scandal.

"Former Enron Chief Financial Officer Andrew S. Fastow Charged with Conspiracy, Wire Fraud, Money Laundering, Conflict of Interest." U.S. Department of Justice, 30 Oct. 2002, https://www.justice.gov/archive/opa/pr/2002/October/02_crm_627.htm.

"Off-balance Sheet Accounting and Manipulation Methods." HowStuffWorks, 15 Aug. 2005, https://money.howstuffworks.com/cooking-books4.htm.

"Red Flags in Enron's Reporting of Revenues and Key Financial Measures." Rice University, http://www.ruf.rice.edu/~bala/files/dharan-bufkins_enron_red_flags.pdf.

"Round-tripping (finance)." Wikipedia, 21 Feb. 2006, https://en.wikipedia.org/wiki/Round-tripping_(finance).

"Round-Trip Trading Definition, Legitimate & Unethical Examples." Investopedia, https://www.investopedia.com/terms/r/round-triptrades.asp.

"SEC v. Andrew S. Fastow." SEC.gov, 20 Aug. 2002, https://www.sec.gov/enforcement-litigation/litigation-releases/lr-17762.

"Special Purpose Entities: Guide to SPEs in Finance." Tavakoli Structured Finance, 12 July 2025, https://www.tavakolistructuredfinance.com/special-purpose-entities/.

"Special Purpose Entities in Commercial Real Estate." Commercial Real Estate Loans, 24 Nov. 2022, https://www.commercialrealestate.loans/commercial-real-estate-glossary/special-purpose-entities/.

"Special-Purpose Entities Are Often." NYU Stern, 20 Feb. 2002, https://pages.stern.nyu.edu/adamodar/New_Home_Page/articles/specpurpentity.htm.

"special purpose entities technical committee." IOSCO, https://www.iosco.org/library/pubdocs/pdf/IOSCOPD243.pdf.

"The Catush Armakkar." The Enron Scandal: A Detailed Overview, 22 July 2024, https://www.catusharmakkar.com/blog/the-enron-scandal-a-detailed-overview.

"The dynamic duo of cognitive dissonance and moral disengagement." ACFE Fraud Magazine, 31 Mar. 2017, https://www.acfe.com/fraud-magazine/all-issues/issue/article?s=2017-april-cognitive-dissonance.

"Understanding Off-Balance Sheet Activities: Types and Key Examples." Investopedia, 24 June 2024, https://www.investopedia.com/terms/o/off-balance-sheet-obs.asp.

"What is a special purpose entity." Central Bank of Ireland, 31 Dec. 2013, https://www.centralbank.ie/consumer-hub/explainers/what-is-a-special-purpose-entity.

Chapter Five

"A History of Corporate Whistleblower Protection Laws and the Efforts to Undermine Them." Whistleblowers Blog, 21 Nov. 2021, https://whistleblowersblog.org/opinion/a-history-of-corporate-whistleblower-protection-laws-and-the-efforts-to-undermine-them/.

"Agency Issues: Shareholders and Corporate Boards." Principles of Finance OpenStax, 13 Apr. 2021, https://pressbooks.ccconline.org/ppscacc2010principlesoffinance/chapter/2-4-agency-issues-shareholders-and-corporate-boards-principles-of-finance-openstax/.

"Agency Problems: Lessons from Enron." LinkedIn, 8 Oct. 2024, https://www.linkedin.com/pulse/agency-problems-lessons-from-enron-mohamed-aboulfadl-2vjzf.

"Corporate Culture." Ethical Systems, 7 Mar. 2021, https://www.ethicalsystems.org/corporate-culture/.

"Enron: an examination of agency problems." Makerere University Business School, https://mubsep.mubs.ac.ug/pluginfile.php/582134/mod_resource/content/0/Enron_An%20example%20of%20the%20Agency%20Problems.pdf.

"Enron and Arthur Andersen: The Case of the Crooked E and the Fallen A." Western Carolina University, https://www.wcu.edu/gpae/Vol3/Enron%20and%20Aurhur%20Andersen.pdf.

"Enron Debacle Example of 'Agency Problem' Within Boards of Directors." University at Buffalo, 22 Jan. 2002, https://www.buffalo.edu/news/releases/2002/01/5523.html.

"Enron." FBI, 18 May 2016, https://www.fbi.gov/history/famous-cases/enron.

"Enron Scandal - Overview, Role of MTM, Agency Conflicts." Corporate Finance Institute, 5 Oct. 2023, https://corporatefinanceinstitute.com/resources/esg/enron-scandal/.

"Enron Scandal and Accounting Fraud: What Happened?" Investopedia, 2 Dec. 2024, https://www.investopedia.com/updates/enron-scandal-summary/.

"Enron scandal." Wikipedia, 5 Feb. 2004, https://en.wikipedia.org/wiki/Enron_scandal.

"Ethics, Corporate Culture, and Compliance." Leading the Way, 29 Mar. 2016, https://opened.tesu.edu/ethicalleadership/chapter/5-2/.

"Ethics in the modern workplace: Lessons from organizational culture and collaboration." University of Pennsylvania, 6 Apr. 2025, https://lpsonline.sas.upenn.edu/features/ethics-modern-workplace-lessons-organizational-culture-and-collaboration.

"Flawed Corporate Cultures Contribution to Corporate Failures or Boards of Directors." LinkedIn, 13 Sept. 2023, https://www.linkedin.com/pulse/flawed-corporate-cultures-contribution-failures-boards-reynolds.

"Former Enron Chief Financial Officer Andrew Fastow Pleads Guilty to Conspiracy to Commit Securities and Wire Fraud." FBI,

13 Jan. 2004, https://www.fbi.gov/news/pressrel/press-releases/former-enron-chief-financial-officer-andrew-fastow-pleads-guilty-to-conspiracy-to-commit-securities-and-wire-fraud.

"Inside this insider trading loophole: What shareholders need to know." Business Think, UNSW, 16 Sept. 2020, https://www.businessthink.unsw.edu.au/articles/insider-trading-loophole-shareholders.

"Lessons from 5 real-life ethical management failures." Ethena, 13 Mar. 2025, https://www.goethena.com/post/5-ethical-management-failures/.

"A List of Recent Major Ethics & Compliance Issues." Ethisphere, 22 May 2025, https://ethisphere.com/major-ethics-compliance-issues-2024-2025/.

"Managing organizational ethics: How ethics becomes pervasive within organizations." PMC, 20 Oct. 2020, https://pmc.ncbi.nlm.nih.gov/articles/PMC7577692/.

"Principal–agent problem." Wikipedia, 15 June 2004, https://en.wikipedia.org/wiki/Principal%E2%80%93agent_problem.

Schery, Allen. Chimpanzee Politics and Moral Cognition: Philosophical Anthropology in Practice. Brooklyn Bridge Books, 2025.

Schery, Allen. The Pattern Seeking Ape: Interdisciplinary Perspectives on Human Cognition and Culture. Brooklyn Bridge Books, 2025.

"The dynamic duo of cognitive dissonance and moral disengagement." ACFE Fraud Magazine, 31 Mar. 2017, https://www.acfe.com/fraud-magazine/all-issues/issue/article?s=2017-april-cognitive-dissonance.

"The Enron Scandal (2001)." International Banker, 28 Sept. 2021, https://internationalbanker.com/history-of-financial-crises/the-enron-scandal-2001/.

Chapter Six

Arendt, Hannah. Between Past and Future: Eight Exercises in Political Thought. Penguin Books, 2006.

Aristotle. Nicomachean Ethics. Translated by Terence Irwin, 2nd ed., Hackett Publishing, 1999.

Cahan, Steven F. Accounting and Auditing Failures: Enron and Beyond. Routledge, 2011.

Coffee, John C. Gatekeepers: The Professions and Corporate Governance. Oxford University Press, 2006.

Foucault, Michel. Discipline and Punish: The Birth of the Prison. Translated by Alan Sheridan, Vintage Books, 1995.

Fuller, Lon L. The Morality of Law. Revised ed., Yale University Press, 1969.

Healy, Paul M., and Krishna G. Palepu. "The Fall of Enron." Journal of Economic Perspectives, vol. 17, no. 2, 2003, pp. 3–26.

McLean, Bethany, and Peter Elkind. The Smartest Guys in the Room: The Amazing Rise and Scandalous Fall of Enron. Portfolio, 2003.

Partnoy, Frank. Infectious Greed: How Deceit and Risk Corrupted the Financial Markets. Henry Holt, 2003.

Polanyi, Karl. The Great Transformation: The Political and Economic Origins of Our Time. Beacon Press, 2001.

Popper, Karl. The Open Society and Its Enemies. Princeton University Press, 2013.

Simon, Herbert A. Administrative Behavior: A Study of Decision-Making Processes in Administrative Organizations. 4th ed., Free Press, 1997.

Smith, Adam. An Inquiry into the Nature and Causes of the Wealth of Nations. Edited by Edwin Cannan, Modern Library, 1994.

Skeel, David A. Icarus in the Boardroom: The Fundamental Flaws in Corporate America and Where They Came From. Oxford University Press, 2005.

Swartz, Mimi, and Sherron Watkins. Power Failure: The Inside Story of the Collapse of Enron. Doubleday, 2003.

Thomas, William A. The Rise and Fall of Enron. Enslow Publishers, 2006.

U.S. Congress. Private Securities Litigation Reform Act of 1995. Public Law 104 67, 109 Stat. 737.

U.S. Senate. The Role of the Board of Directors in Enron's Collapse. Report prepared by the Permanent Subcommittee on Inve

Chapter Seven

Blind Faith: How Deregulation and Enron's Influence Over Government Looted Billions from Americans. Public Citizen, Dec. 2001. https://www.citizen.org/wp-content/uploads/blind_faith.pdf.

"Energy Trader Admits Faking Transactions." The New York Times, 14 May 2002. https://www.nytimes.com/2002/05/14/business/energy-trader-admits-faking-transactions.html.

Enron: Not Accounting for the Future. Harbert College of Business, Auburn University. https://harbert.auburn.edu/binaries/documents/center-for-ethical-organizational-cultures/cases/enron.pdf.

"Enron scandal." Encyclopædia Britannica, 25 Sept. 2025. https://www.britannica.com/event/Enron-scandal.

"Enron Scandal and Accounting Fraud: What Happened?" Investopedia, 2 Dec. 2024. https://www.investopedia.com/updates/enron-scandal-summary/.

"Enron Scandal – Overview, Role of MTM, Agency Conflicts." Corporate Finance Institute, 5 Oct. 2023. https://corporatefinanceinstitute.com/resources/esg/enron-scandal/.

"Enron: An Accounting Scandal That Changed Everything." Encoursa™, 1 May 2023. https://encoursa.com/blog/zp3wpy26/enron-an-accounting-scandal-that-changed-everything.

"How Have Business Ethics Evolved Over Time?" Investopedia, 20 Mar. 2025. https://www.investopedia.com/ask/answers/022615/how-have-business-ethics-evolved-over-time.asp.

"Management Controls: The Organizational Fraud Triangle of Leadership, Culture and Control in Enron." Ivey Business Journal, 23 Feb. 2015. https://iveybusinessjournal.com/publication/management-controls-the-organizational-fraud-triangle-of-leadership-culture-and-control-in-enron/.

Off-Balance Sheet Accounting and Manipulation Methods. HowStuffWorks, 15 Aug. 2005. https://money.howstuffworks.com/cooking-books4.htm.

"Private Securities Litigation Reform Act of 1995," Pub. L. No. 104-67, 109 Stat. 737.

Sarbanes-Oxley Act of 2002, Pub. L. No. 107-204, 116 Stat. 745.

"The Dynamic Duo of Cognitive Dissonance and Moral Disengagement." ACFE Fraud Magazine, 31 Mar. 2017. https://www.acfe.com/fraud-magazine/all-issues/issue/article?s=2017-april-cognitive-dissonance.

"The Enron Collapse: Compliance Failures and Lessons." Planet Compliance, 27 Apr. 2025. https://www.planetcompliance.com/soc-2/enron-collapse-compliance/.

"The Enron Trial: A Chronology." Famous Trials, 22 Jan. 2002. https://famous-trials.com/enron/1789-chronology.

"The Sarbanes-Oxley Act at Fifteen: A Brief Overview." U.S. Securities and Exchange Commission. https://www.sec.gov/about/laws/soa2002.pdf.

"Timeline: Ken Lay and the Arc of Enron." NPR, 5 July 2006. https://www.npr.org/2006/07/05/5535821/timeline-ken-lay-and-the-arc-of-enron.

Chapter Eight

"Agenda-Setting Theory and Access Journalism." Journalism Studies, vol. 12, no. 4, 2011, pp. 497–513.

"Enron Collapse Spurs Financial Reform." Congressional Record, 24 July 2002.

Enron: Not Accounting for the Future. Harbert College of Business, Auburn University. https://harbert.auburn.edu/binaries/documents/center-for-ethical-organizational-cultures/cases/enron.pdf.

"Financial Stability Board Principles for Sound Compensation Practices." FSB, Apr. 2009, https://www.fsb.org/wp-content/uploads/r_0904b.pdf.

"How Have Business Ethics Evolved Over Time?" Investopedia, 20 Mar. 2025, https://www.investopedia.com/ask/answers/022615/how-have-business-ethics-evolved-over-time.asp.

"International Organization of Securities Commissions (IOSCO) Technical Committee Special Purpose Entities." IOSCO, 2002, https://www.iosco.org/library/pubdocs/pdf/IOSCOPD243.pdf.

"Principles of Corporate Governance." OECD, 2004, https://www.oecd.org/daf/ca/corporategovernanceprinciples/31557724.pdf.

Public Company Accounting Oversight Board. "About the PCAOB." PCAOB, https://pcaobus.org/About/Pages/default.aspx.

Sarbanes-Oxley Act of 2002, Pub. L. No. 107-204, 116 Stat. 745.

"SEC Interpretation: Commission Guidance Regarding Management's Discussion and Analysis of Financial Condition and Results of Operations." SEC Release No. 33-8350, Dec. 19, 2003.

"Stakeholder Theory of the Modern Corporation." Business Ethics Quarterly, vol. 17, no. 4, 2007, pp. 541–63.

"Ten Years of Enron: Lessons Learned." Planet Compliance, 8 Dec. 2011, https://www.planetcompliance.com/soc-2/enron-collapse-compliance/.

"Toward Global Convergence of Accounting Standards." International Accounting Standards Board,

2002, https://www.ifrs.org/content/dam/ifrs/publications/pdf-standards/2002/IASB_Toward_Global_Convergence.pdf.

Whistleblowers Should Avoid Internal Reporting Channels. Whistleblowers.org, 18 Apr. 2021, https://www.whistleblowers.org/internal-reporting-channels/.

"World Bank Principles of Corporate Governance." World Bank, 1999, http://documents.worldbank.org/curated/en/476301468762815153/Corporate-governance-principles-guidelines-and-code-of-conduct.

Chapter Nine

European Commission. Action Plan: Modernising Company Law and Enhancing Corporate Governance in the European Union. Brussels, 2003.

Financial Reporting Council. UK Corporate Governance Code 2018. Financial Reporting Council, 2018.

German Corporate Governance Code Commission. German Corporate Governance Code. As amended 28 Apr. 2022.

International Accounting Standards Board (IASB). International Financial Reporting Standards (IFRS): Conceptual Framework for Financial Reporting. IFRS Foundation, 2018.

International Organization of Securities Commissions (IOSCO). Report on Corporate Governance. FR10/16, Oct. 2016.

Lawson v. FMR LLC, 571 U.S. 429 (2014).

Murray v. UBS Securities, LLC, 601 U.S. \_\_\_ (2024).

Romano, Roberta. "The Sarbanes Oxley Act and the Making of Quack Corporate Governance." Yale Law Journal, vol. 114, no. 7, 2005, pp. 1521–1611.

Sarbanes Oxley Act of 2002, Pub. L. 107 204, 116 Stat. 745 (2002).

United States, Supreme Court. Free Enterprise Fund v. Public Company Accounting Oversight Board, 561 U.S. 477 (2010).

United States, Supreme Court. Yates v. United States, 574 U.S. 528 (2015).

U.S. Securities and Exchange Commission. Report Pursuant to Section 704 of the Sarbanes Oxley Act of 2002. SEC, 2003.

Steinberg, Marc I., and A.B. Steinberg. "Unflexed Muscle: SEC Enforcement of CEO and CFO SOX Certifications." CLS Blue Sky Blog, 27 Mar. 2025.

U.S. Government Accountability Office. Sarbanes Oxley Act: Compliance Costs Are Higher for Larger Companies but More Burdensome for Smaller Ones. GAO 25 107500, June 2025.

Federal Energy Regulatory Commission. Staff White Paper on Anti Market Manipulation Enforcement Efforts Ten Years After EPAct 2005. Nov. 2016.

Hartman, Devin. "Exorcising the Ghosts of Enron." R Street Institute, 29 July 2024.

Bonneville Power Administration. "How Two FERC Orders Revolutionized the Power Utility Industry." BPA Newsroom, 20 Dec. 2024.

Chapter Ten

Bandura, Albert. "The Dynamic Duo of Cognitive Dissonance and Moral Disengagement." ACFE Fraud Magazine, 31 Mar. 2017, https://www.acfe.com/fraud-magazine/all-issues/issue/article?s=2017-april-cognitive-dissonance.

Festinger, Leon. A Theory of Cognitive Dissonance. Stanford UP, 1957.

Haidt, Jonathan. The Righteous Mind: Why Good People Are Divided by Politics and Religion. Pantheon Books, 2012.

Hawkes, Kristen, and Richard Jones. "Hadza Men's Foraging Goals and Preferences for Sharing." Evolution and Human Behavior, vol. 17, no. 2, 1996, pp. 81–97.

Turner, Victor W. The Ritual Process: Structure and Anti-Structure. Aldine Transaction, 1969.

Wason, Peter C. "Reasoning About a Rule." Quarterly Journal of Experimental Psychology, vol. 20, no. 3, 1968, pp. 273–81.

Wilson, David Sloan. Darwin's Cathedral: Evolution, Religion, and the Nature of Society. University of Chicago Press 2002

Chapter Eleven

Ammous, Saifedean. The Bitcoin Standard: The Decentralized Alternative to Central Banking. Wiley, 2018.

Arora, Payal. "Algorithmic Accountability: A Primer." Communications of the ACM, vol. 62, no. 6, 2019, pp. 30–32.

Bandura, Albert. "The Dynamic Duo of Cognitive Dissonance and Moral Disengagement." ACFE Fraud Magazine, 31 Mar. 2017, https://www.acfe.com/fraud-magazine/all-issues/issue/article?s=2017-april-cognitive-dissonance.

Brynjolfsson, Erik, and Andrew McAfee. The Second Machine Age: Work, Progress, and Prosperity in a Time of Brilliant Technologies. W. W. Norton, 2014.

Buterin, Vitalik. "DAOs, DACs, DAs and More: An Incomplete Terminology Guide." Ethereum Blog, 6 May 2014, https://blog.ethereum.org/2014/05/06/daos-dacs-das-and-more-an-incomplete-terminology-guide/.

Fischer, Patrick, and Emmanouil Mentzakis. "Smart Contracts and Their Application in the Financial Sector." Journal of Digital Banking, vol. 3, no. 2, 2018, pp. 121–32.

Floridi, Luciano. The Ethics of Information. Oxford University Press, 2013.

Gartner. "Magic Quadrant for Data Science and Machine-Learning Platforms." 2020, https://www.gartner.com/document/3981869?ref=solrResearch&refval=222732173&qid=bd9166e7770dfb3e70b4312f2bb20f12.

Jobin, Anna, Marcello Ienca, and Effy Vayena. "The Global Landscape of AI Ethics Guidelines." Nature Machine Intelligence, vol. 1, no. 9, 2019, pp. 389–99.

Meadows, Donella H., et al. Thinking in Systems: A Primer. Chelsea Green Publishing, 2008.

Nakamoto, Satoshi. "Bitcoin: A Peer-to-Peer Electronic Cash System." 2008. Bitcoin.org, https://bitcoin.org/bitcoin.pdf.

O'Neil, Cathy. Weapons of Math Destruction: How Big Data Increases Inequality and Threatens Democracy. Crown, 2016.

Szabo, Nick. "Formalizing and Securing Relationships on Public Networks." First Monday, vol. 2, no. 9, 1997, https://firstmonday.org/article/view/548/469.

Tapscott, Don, and Alex Tapscott. Blockchain Revolution: How the Technology Behind Bitcoin and Other Cryptocurrencies Is Changing the World. Portfolio, 2016.

Wood, Gavin. "Ethereum: A Secure Decentralised Generalised Transaction Ledger." Ethereum Foundation, 2014, https://ethereum.github.io/yellowpaper/paper.pdf.

Chapter Twelve

Energy Policy Act of 1992, Pub. L. No. 102-486, 106 Stat. 2776.

Nakamoto, Satoshi. "Bitcoin: A Peer-to-Peer Electronic Cash System." 2008, Bitc. 29, 2002.

"Wall Street Journal: 'Enron's Sharper Accounting Faces Scrutiny,'" Oct. 16, 2001.

Wood, Gavin. "Ethereum: A Secure Decentralised Generalised Transaction Ledger." Ethereum Foundation, 2014, https://ethereum.github.io/yellowpaper/paper.pdfoin.org, https://bitcoin.org/bitcoin.pdf.

"Private Securities Litigation Reform Act of 1995," Pub. L. No. 104-67, 109 Stat. 737.

Sarbanes-Oxley Act of 2002, Pub. L. No. 107-204, 116 Stat. 745.

"Telecommunications Act of 1996," Pub. L. No. 104-104, 110 Stat. 56.

Testimony of Sherron Watkins before the Senate Committee on Governmental Affairs,

# Index

**A**

accountability, corporate, 100–101

accounting fraud, 108

AI, 138, 141–42, 144–45

AI design, ethical, 143

AI ethics guidelines, 148

AI model drift, 145

AI models, 143–44

American corporate history, 3

American culture, 123

anthropological insights, 105, 124, 138

anthropological perspective, philosophical, 21, 50

Anthropological Reflections, 117

Anthropological research, 12, 127

anthropological studies, 120, 132

anthropological understanding, 101, 107

arbitrage, regulatory, 15, 27, 118, 122

Arthur Andersen, 11, 33

**B**
balance sheets, 13, 32, 98
bankruptcy, 16, 97–98, 148
biases, models risk replicating, 138
blockchain, 137–38, 141–42, 144–45
 permissioned, 137, 142
blockchain ethics calls, 140
blockchain governance models, 139
breakdown, ethical, 17
business ethics, 3, 8, 99
business innovation, 28, 147
business models, 15, 22, 25, 29, 51, 58, 68, 80
 abstract, 25
 revolutionary, 126

**C**
cognition, 130, 132, 150, 152
 moral, 132
Cognitive Bias Activation, 129
cognitive biases, 52, 102, 104, 120, 129, 134
cognitive blind spots, 135

cognitive dimensions, 134

cognitive factors, 100

collusion, 53–54

company, rogue, 63, 75

company bankruptcy, 58

company stock, 98

compass, 69, 81

competitive advantage, 25, 121

complex abstractions, 118

complex dealmaking, 123

complex international stage, 15

corporate environments, complex, 129

corporate excess, 10

corporate goals, 8

corporate governance, 99, 102, 106, 116, 135, 142, 148, 150

corporate governance systems, 50, 61

corporate health, 14

corporate malfeasance, 95

corporate scandals, 17, 19, 61, 113

corruption, corporate, 1, 50, 61

cultural alignment, 135

cultural disintegration, 97

cultural dynamics, 134

cultural evolution, 29

cultural narratives, 123, 125, 134, 153

cultural norms, 107, 120, 124

cultural transformation, 61–62

## D

deception, 1, 18, 36, 63, 73, 75, 85, 120, 123
 corporate, 71, 83

deregulation, wave of, 64, 76

design
 ethical, 141, 145
 value-sensitive, 140, 148

Designing Cultures, 132

detection, anomaly, 140–41, 149

dissent, 7, 12, 55, 71, 83, 113, 123, 128, 133

dissonance, cognitive, 121, 129

dissonance theory, 59, 126

## E

energy business, 21

energy sector, 19, 25, 105

energy trading, pioneered, 65, 77

Enron agency failures, 62

Enron board, 56
Enron business model, 54, 59
Enron case, 35, 125, 141
Enron's collapse, 16–17, 134
Enron shareholders, 53–54
Enron's leadership, 127, 139
Enron stock, 54, 98
ethical behavior, 132
ethical boundaries blur, 121
ethical commands, 31
ethical complexities, 134
ethical compromise, 28
ethical considerations, 8–9, 55, 133, 140
ethical decision-making, 57, 133
ethical guidelines, 144
ethical huddles, 133
ethical lapses, 3
ethical outcomes, 139
ethical oversight, 55
ethical rules, 9
ethical sensitivity, 132
ethicists, 144
ethics, 118, 121, 124, 132, 134, 139, 148, 151, 153

corporate, 100

legislating, 114

executive compensation, 27, 52

F

failures

critical, 68, 80

technical, 69, 81

fragmentation, 118–19, 124

fraud, systemic, 129, 141

G

governance, 70, 82, 141, 145–46, 152

group cognition, 125, 128–29

H

Historical Regulatory, 1, 75

history, corporate, 24, 150

human cognition, 141, 151

human evolution, 129

human evolutionary gifts, 135

human feedback, 138

human ingenuity, 125

human limitations, 71, 83

human mind paintings, 74, 86

human survival, 120

human values, 143

I

ideology, free-market, 3

incentive structures, 50, 107, 132

incentive systems, 129, 132, 139

K

Key Players, 1, 30

L

landscapes, moral, 123

language, moral, 131

Lay, 18–21

leadership, visionary, 18

leadership behavior, 55

legitimate business purpose, 59

loyalty, in-group, 16, 55

M

management decisions, 56

market capitalization, 16, 28

Mark-to-Market, 37

misconduct, corporate, 10, 141

moral anchors, 132

moral canvas, 150

moral defaults, 153

moral dilemmas, 35

moral dispositions, 124

moral hazard, 13

morality, 123, 140, 150–52

N

natural gas, 65, 72, 77, 84

norms, 115, 127–28

 moral, 120

O

Oovernance models, 134

opacity, 6, 24–25, 51, 64, 76, 107

opportunism, 122, 124, 134

organizational designs, 22, 125

## P

power, 19, 21, 74, 86, 107, 111, 113, 143

pragmatism, moral, 121, 123–24

pressure, 8, 10, 12, 21, 31, 52, 56, 73, 85, 101, 113, 135

principal-agent theory, 50

professional skepticism, 57, 101, 103

## R

reforms, corporate, 109

resources, limited, 11, 58

response, neurological, 9, 58

risk management infrastructure, 27

risks, monitored market, 117

## S

safeguards, structural, 132–33

Sarbanes Oxley Act, 1, 108

securities fraud, 89, 147

sentinel awareness, 5, 117, 120, 124

shareholder interests, 99, 104

shareholder lawsuits, 66, 78

Skilling, 8, 12, 14–15, 100

small-scale societies, 55, 124–25

speculative trading, 26, 105

standards, ethical, 32, 126

## T

technological innovations, 135, 143, 153

technological solutions, 124, 137, 140

token-based voting, 143, 145

tribal loyalty, 50, 126–29, 133

## V

vulnerabilities, systemic, 29

## W

whistleblower protections, 101, 109, 113

[Created with TExtract / www.TExtract.com]